DANIEL X

ALIEN HUNTER

JAMES
PATTERSON
& LEOPOLDO GOUT

ART BY
KLAUS LYNGELED
JON GIRIN & JOSEPH McLAMB

LITTLE, BROWN AND COMPANY
HACHETTE BOOK GROUP USA
237 PARK AVENUE, NEW YORK, NY 10017

VISIT OUR WEB SITE AT
WWW.HACHETTEBOOKGROUPUSA.COM

FIRST EDITION: DECEMBER 2008

FRONT COVER ART BY JON GIRIN
BACK COVER ART BY KLAUS LYNGELED

ISBN: 978 0 316 00425 1

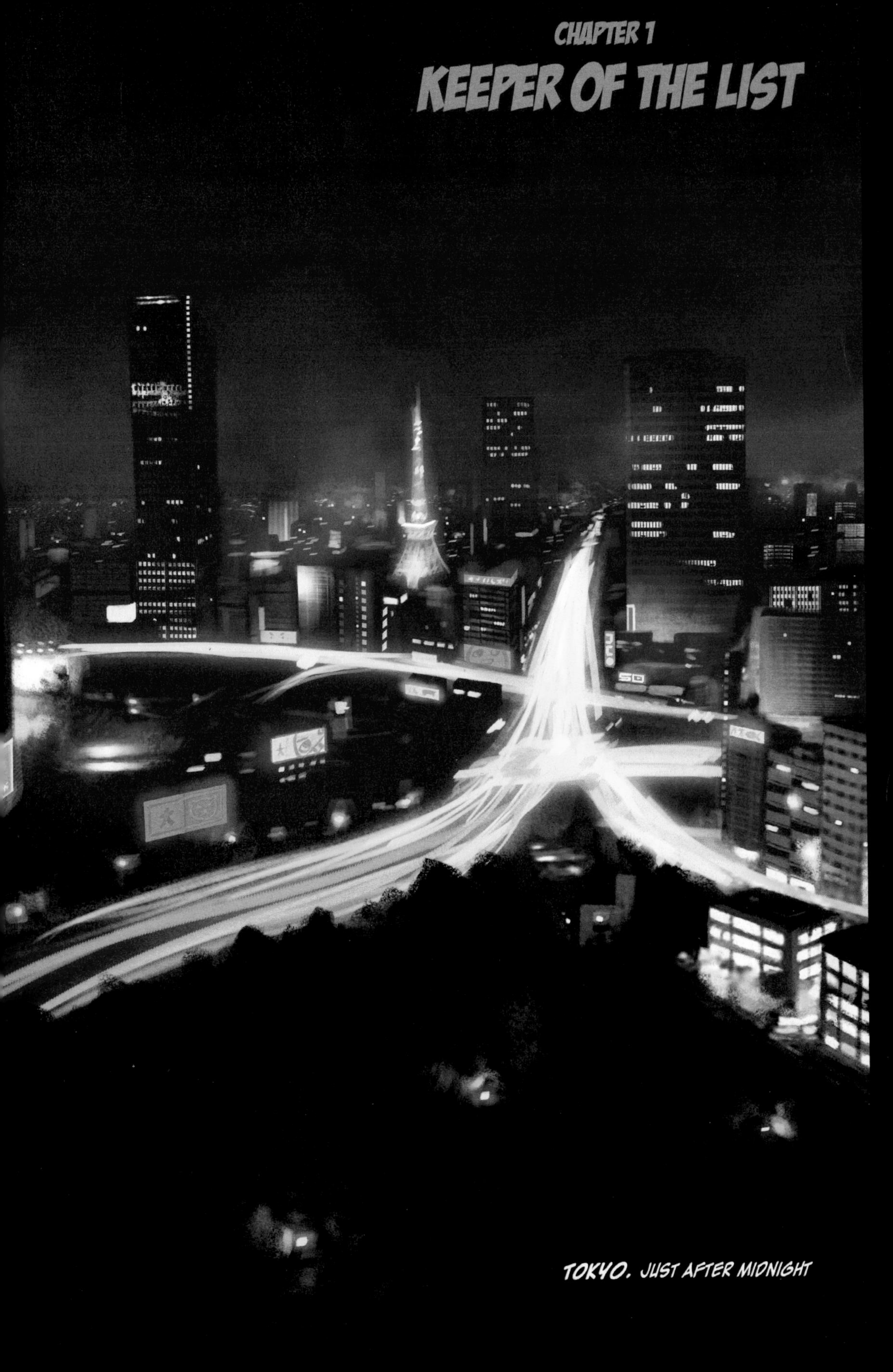
CHAPTER 1
KEEPER OF THE LIST
TOKYO. JUST AFTER MIDNIGHT

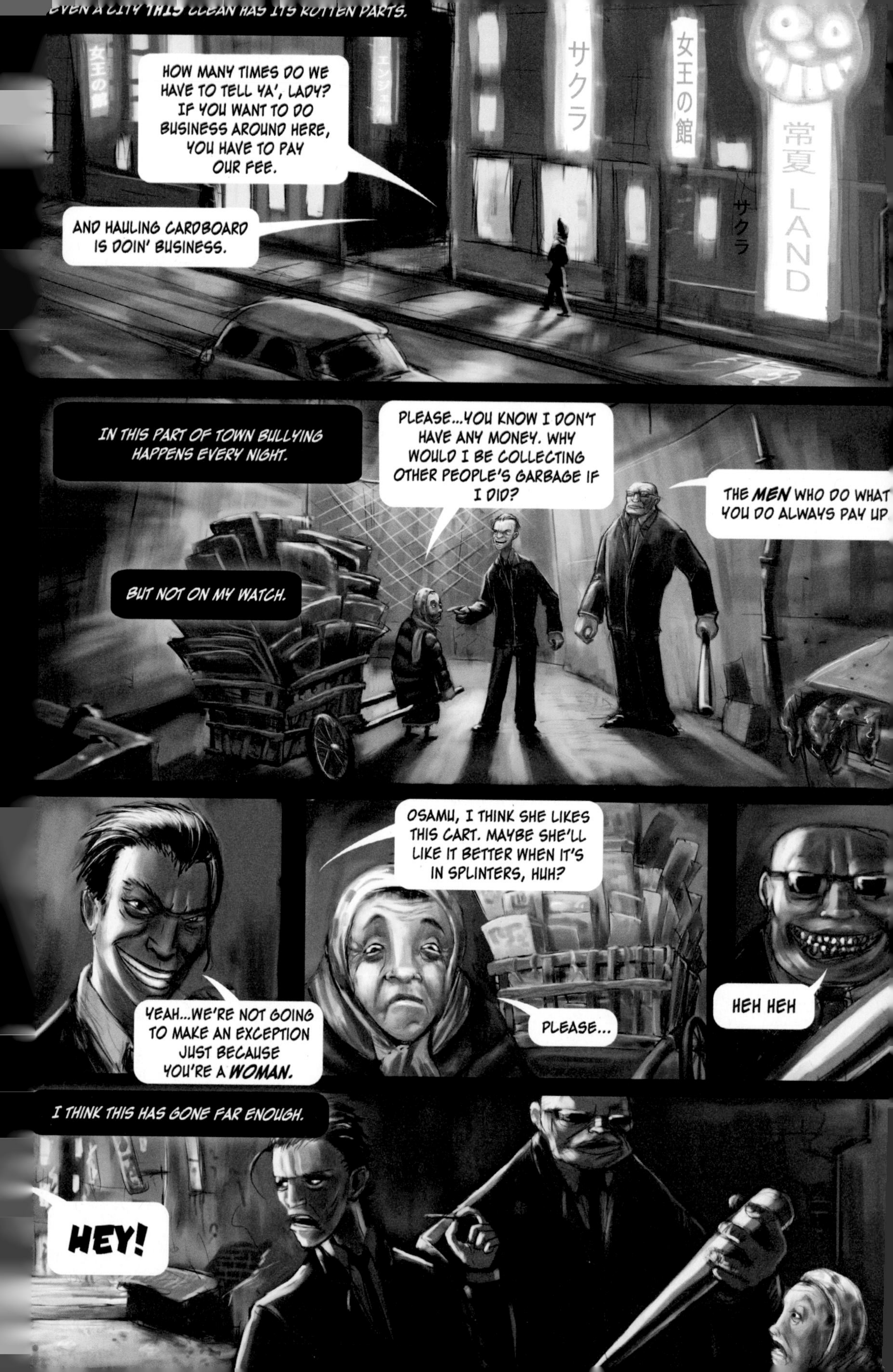
EVEN A CITY THIS CLEAN HAS ITS ROTTEN PARTS.
サクラ
女王の館
常夏 LAND
サクラ
HOW MANY TIMES DO WE HAVE TO TELL YA', LADY? IF YOU WANT TO DO BUSINESS AROUND HERE, YOU HAVE TO PAY OUR FEE.
AND HAULING CARDBOARD IS DOIN' BUSINESS.
IN THIS PART OF TOWN BULLYING HAPPENS EVERY NIGHT.
PLEASE...YOU KNOW I DON'T HAVE ANY MONEY. WHY WOULD I BE COLLECTING OTHER PEOPLE'S GARBAGE IF I DID?
THE MEN WHO DO WHAT YOU DO ALWAYS PAY UP.
BUT NOT ON MY WATCH.
YEAH...WE'RE NOT GOING TO MAKE AN EXCEPTION JUST BECAUSE YOU'RE A WOMAN.
OSAMU, I THINK SHE LIKES THIS CART. MAYBE SHE'LL LIKE IT BETTER WHEN IT'S IN SPLINTERS, HUH?
PLEASE...
HEH HEH
I THINK THIS HAS GONE FAR ENOUGH.
HEY!

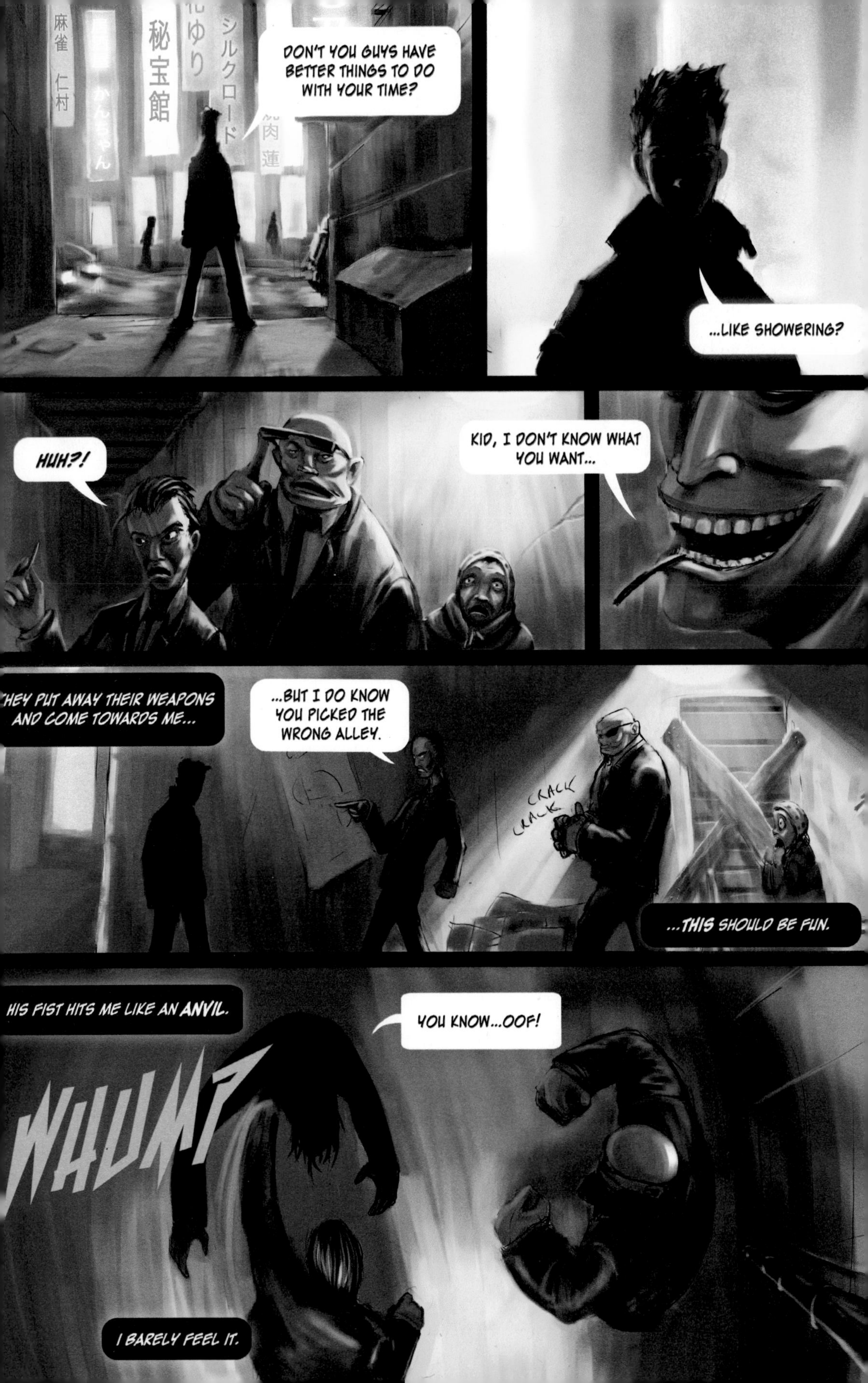
麻雀
仁村
秘宝館
シルクロード
かんちゃん
DON'T YOU GUYS HAVE BETTER THINGS TO DO WITH YOUR TIME?
...LIKE SHOWERING?
HUH?!
KID, I DON'T KNOW WHAT YOU WANT...
HEY PUT AWAY THEIR WEAPONS AND COME TOWARDS ME...
...BUT I DO KNOW YOU PICKED THE WRONG ALLEY.
CRACK
CRACK
...THIS SHOULD BE FUN.
HIS FIST HITS ME LIKE AN ANVIL.
YOU KNOW...OOF!
WHUMP
I BARELY FEEL IT.

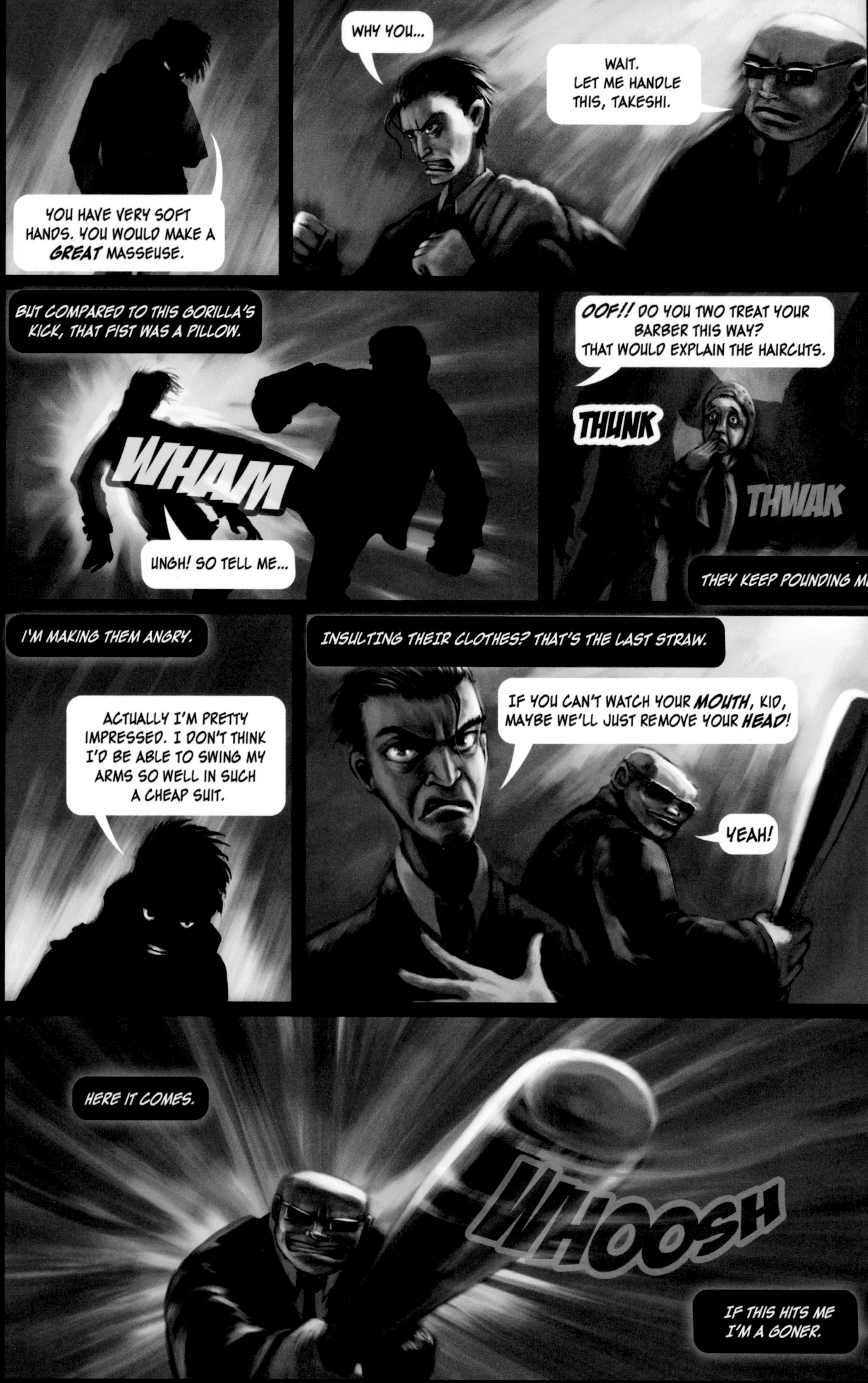
YOU HAVE VERY SOFT HANDS. YOU WOULD MAKE A GREAT MASSEUSE.
WHY YOU...
WAIT. LET ME HANDLE THIS, TAKESHI.
BUT COMPARED TO THIS GORILLA'S KICK, THAT FIST WAS A PILLOW.
WHAM
UNGH! SO TELL ME...
OOF!! DO YOU TWO TREAT YOUR BARBER THIS WAY? THAT WOULD EXPLAIN THE HAIRCUTS.
THUNK
THWAK
THEY KEEP POUNDING M
I'M MAKING THEM ANGRY.
ACTUALLY I'M PRETTY IMPRESSED. I DON'T THINK I'D BE ABLE TO SWING MY ARMS SO WELL IN SUCH A CHEAP SUIT.
INSULTING THEIR CLOTHES? THAT'S THE LAST STRAW.
IF YOU CAN'T WATCH YOUR MOUTH, KID, MAYBE WE'LL JUST REMOVE YOUR HEAD!
YEAH!
HERE IT COMES.
WHOOSH
IF THIS HITS ME I'M A GONER.

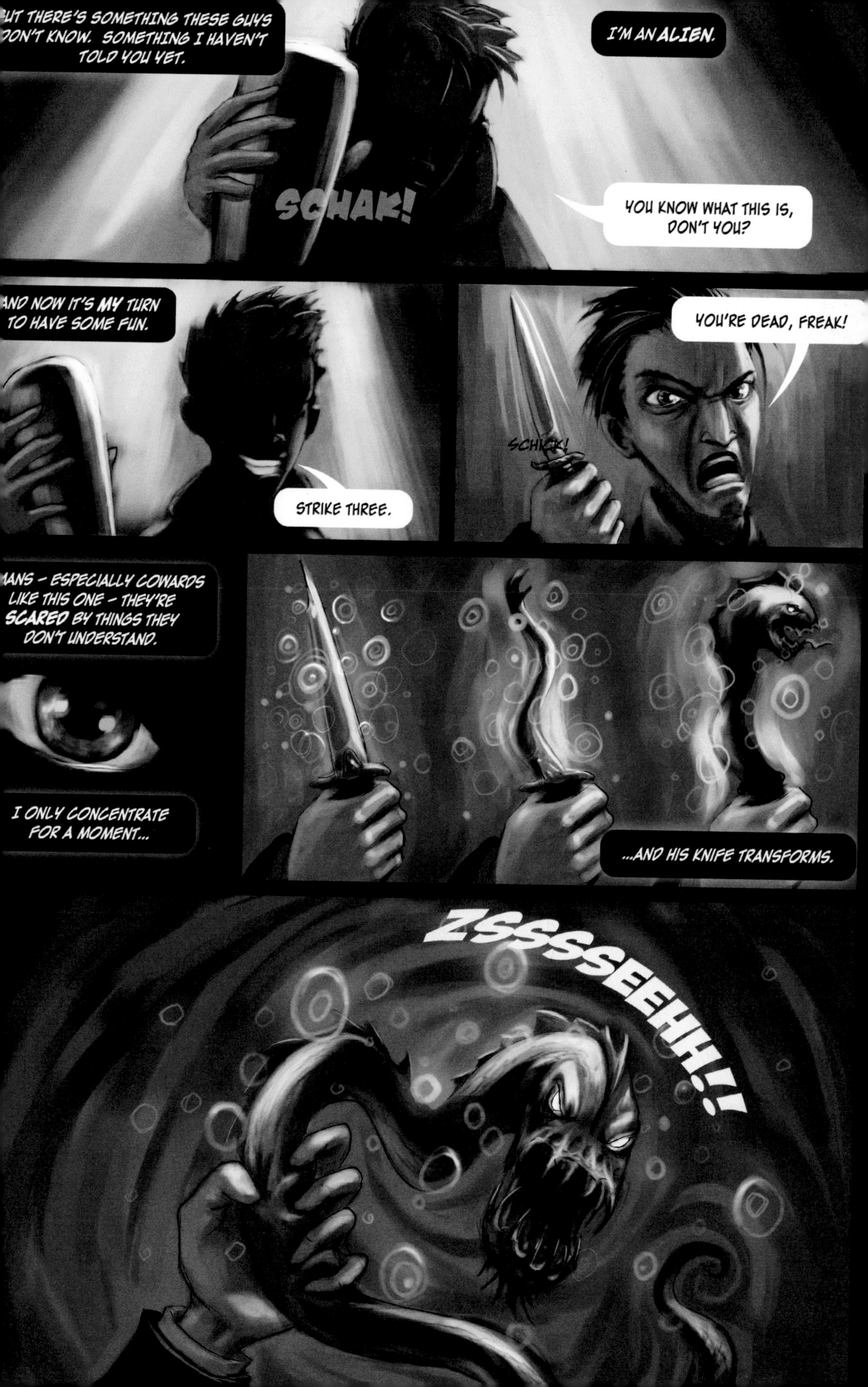
UT THERE'S SOMETHING THESE GUYS DON'T KNOW. SOMETHING I HAVEN'T TOLD YOU YET.
I'M AN ALIEN.
SCHAK!
YOU KNOW WHAT THIS IS, DON'T YOU?
AND NOW IT'S MY TURN TO HAVE SOME FUN.
STRIKE THREE.
YOU'RE DEAD, FREAK!
SCHICK!
MANS – ESPECIALLY COWARDS LIKE THIS ONE – THEY'RE SCARED BY THINGS THEY DON'T UNDERSTAND.
I ONLY CONCENTRATE FOR A MOMENT...
...AND HIS KNIFE TRANSFORMS.
ZSSSSEEHH!!

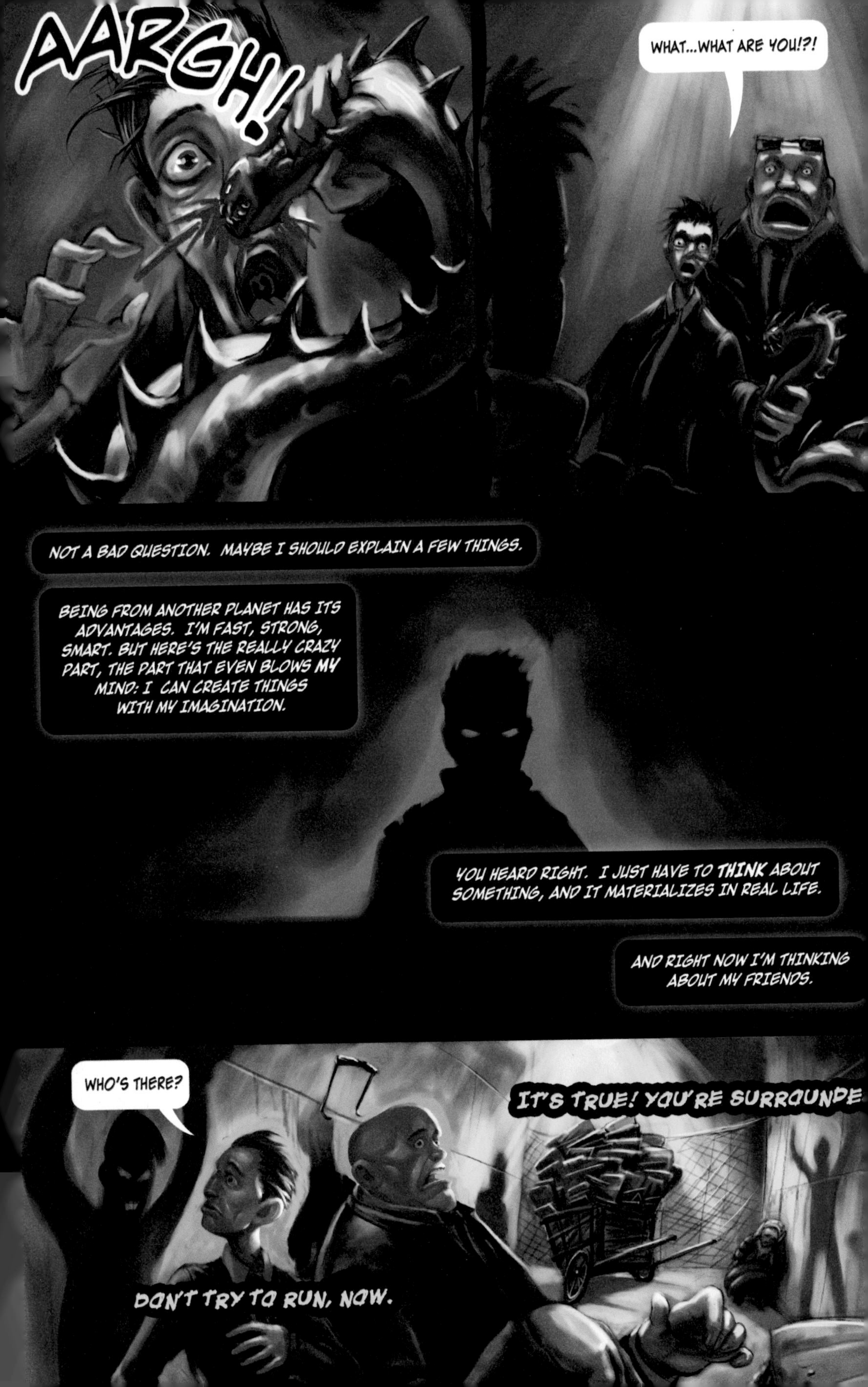
AARGH!!
WHAT...WHAT ARE YOU!?!
NOT A BAD QUESTION. MAYBE I SHOULD EXPLAIN A FEW THINGS.
BEING FROM ANOTHER PLANET HAS ITS ADVANTAGES. I'M FAST, STRONG, SMART. BUT HERE'S THE REALLY CRAZY PART, THE PART THAT EVEN BLOWS MY MIND: I CAN CREATE THINGS WITH MY IMAGINATION.
YOU HEARD RIGHT. I JUST HAVE TO THINK ABOUT SOMETHING, AND IT MATERIALIZES IN REAL LIFE.
AND RIGHT NOW I'M THINKING ABOUT MY FRIENDS.
WHO'S THERE?
IT'S TRUE! YOU'RE SURROUNDE
DON'T TRY TO RUN, NOW.

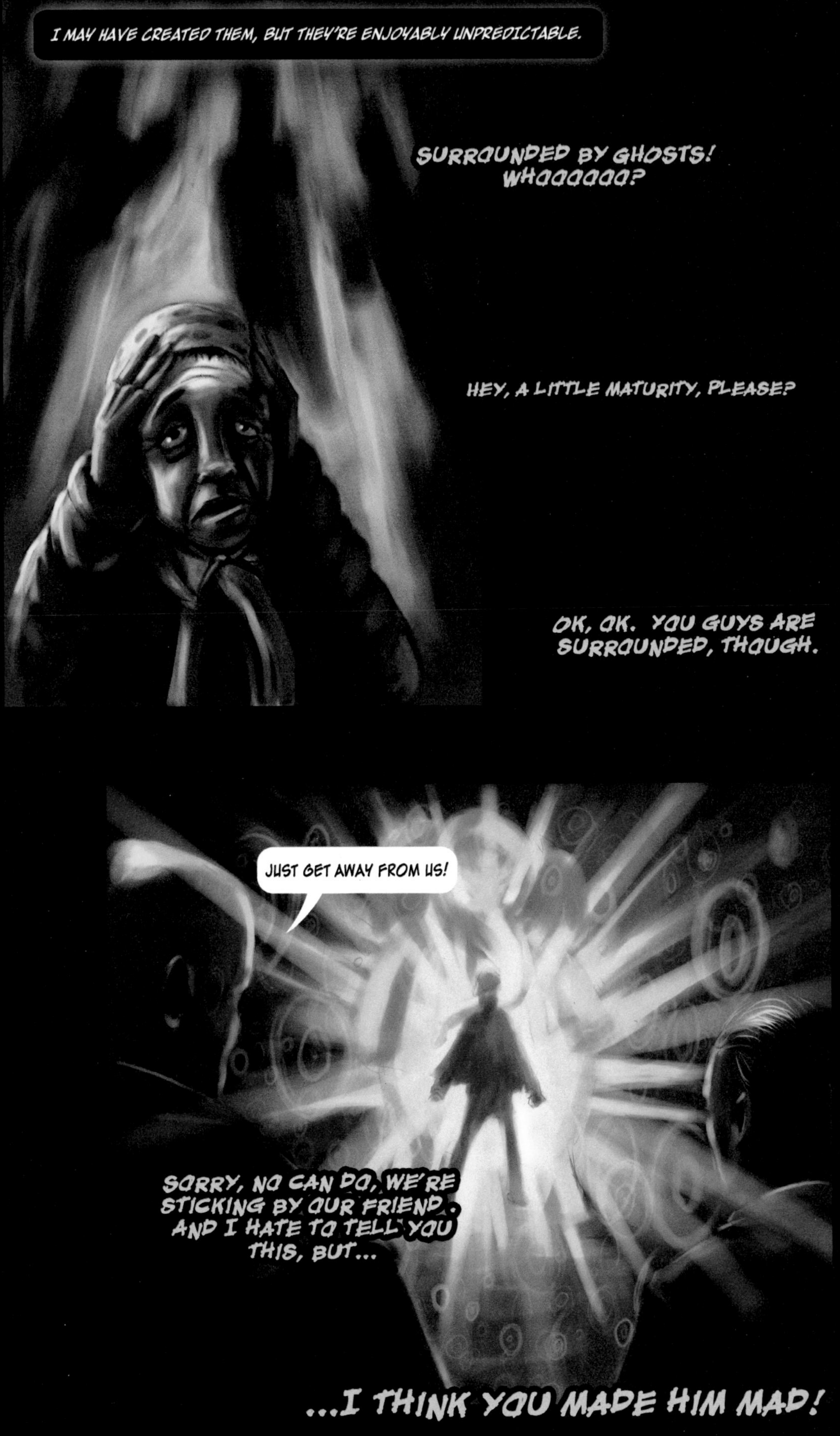
I MAY HAVE CREATED THEM, BUT THEY'RE ENJOYABLY UNPREDICTABLE.
SURROUNDED BY GHOSTS! WHAAAAAA?
HEY, A LITTLE MATURITY, PLEASE?
OK, OK. YOU GUYS ARE SURROUNDED, THOUGH.
JUST GET AWAY FROM US!
SORRY, NO CAN DO, WE'RE STICKING BY OUR FRIEND. AND I HATE TO TELL YOU THIS, BUT...
...I THINK YOU MADE HIM MAD!

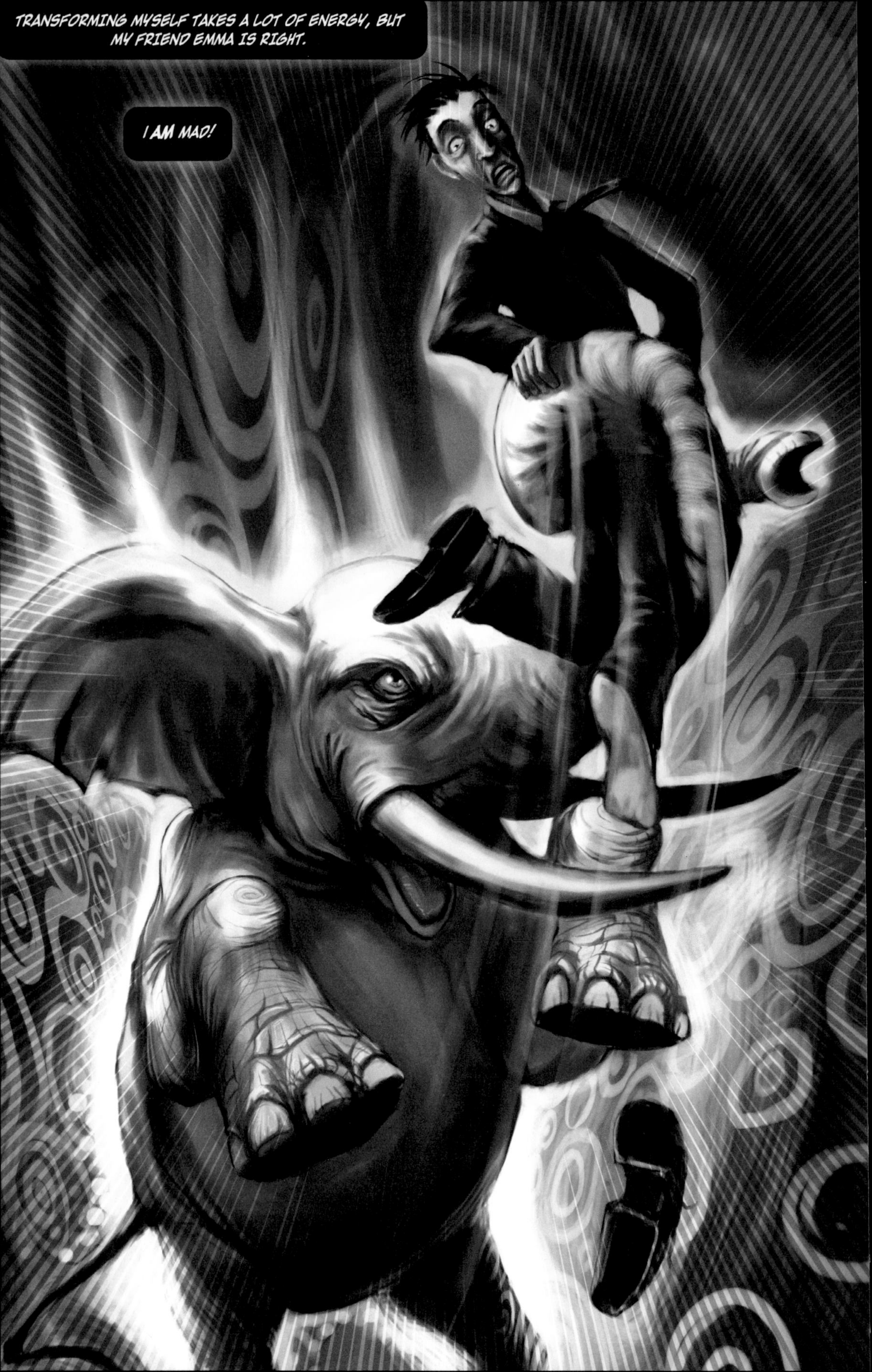
TRANSFORMING MYSELF TAKES A LOT OF ENERGY, BUT MY FRIEND EMMA IS RIGHT.
I AM MAD!

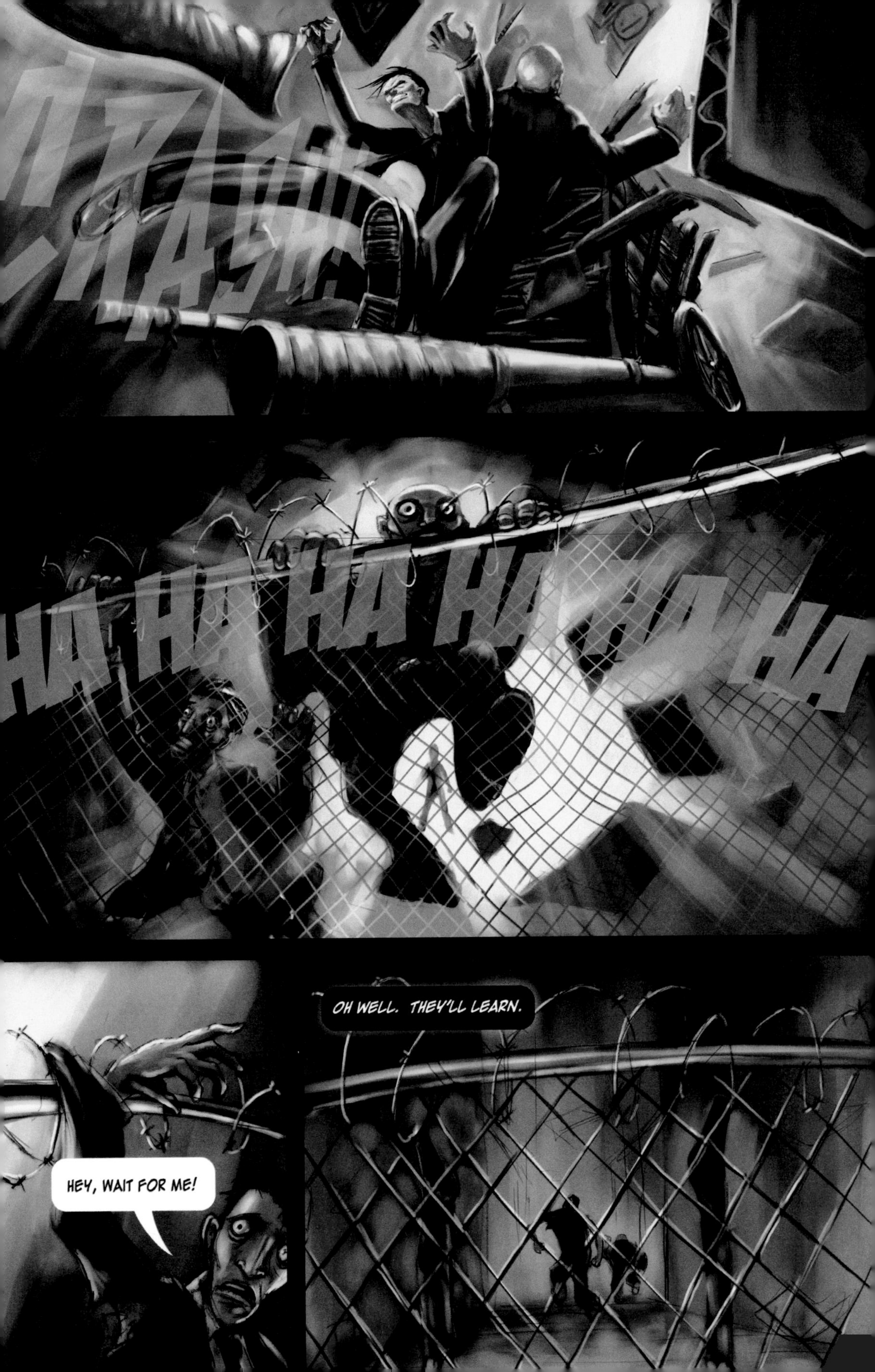
CRASH!
HA HA HA HA HA HA
OH WELL. THEY'LL LEARN.
HEY, WAIT FOR ME!

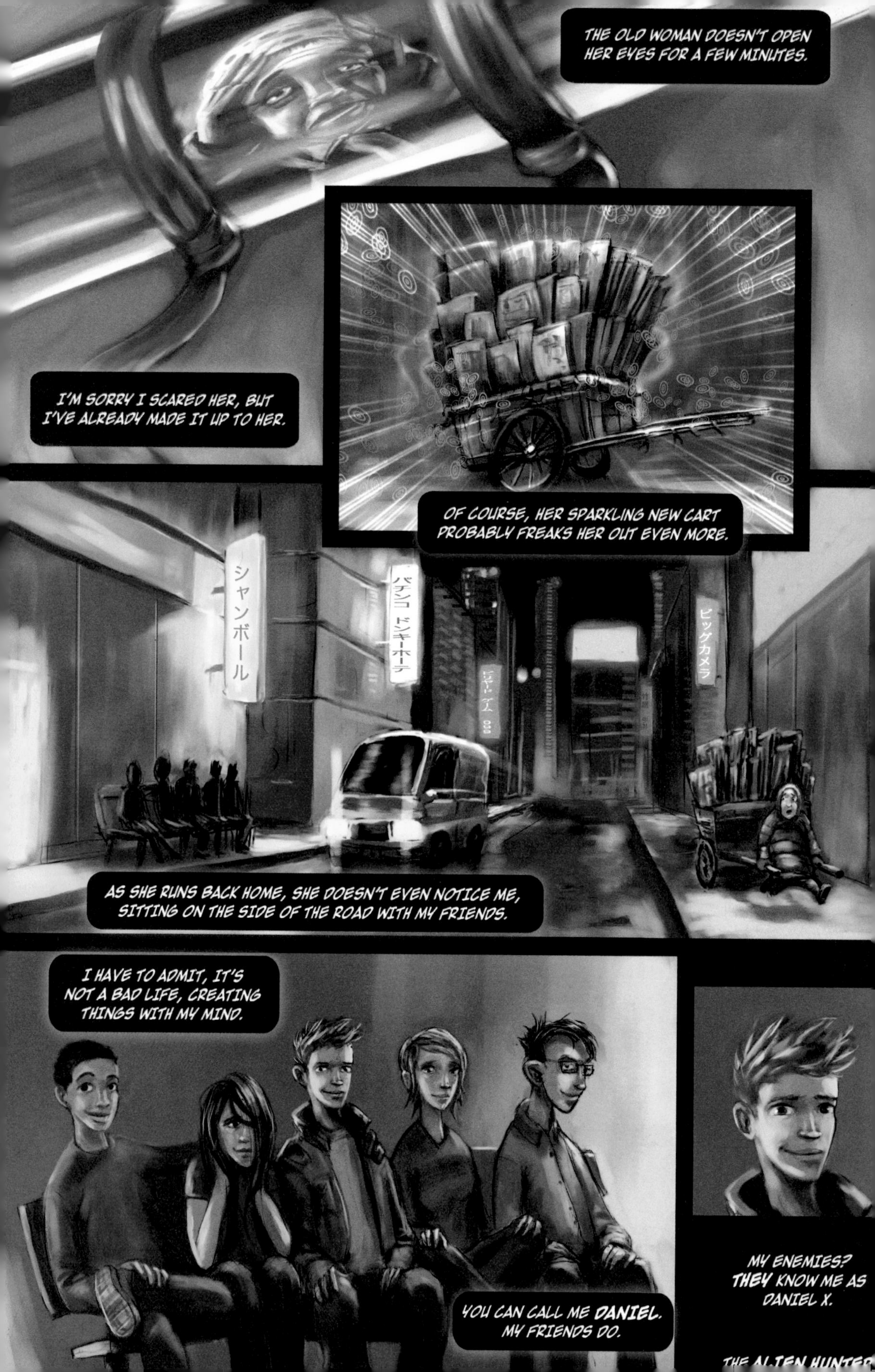
THE OLD WOMAN DOESN'T OPEN HER EYES FOR A FEW MINUTES.
I'M SORRY I SCARED HER, BUT I'VE ALREADY MADE IT UP TO HER.
OF COURSE, HER SPARKLING NEW CART PROBABLY FREAKS HER OUT EVEN MORE.
シャンボール
パチンコ ドンキーホーテ
ビッグカメラ
AS SHE RUNS BACK HOME, SHE DOESN'T EVEN NOTICE ME, SITTING ON THE SIDE OF THE ROAD WITH MY FRIENDS.
I HAVE TO ADMIT, IT'S NOT A BAD LIFE, CREATING THINGS WITH MY MIND.
YOU CAN CALL ME DANIEL. MY FRIENDS DO.
MY ENEMIES? THEY KNOW ME AS DANIEL X.

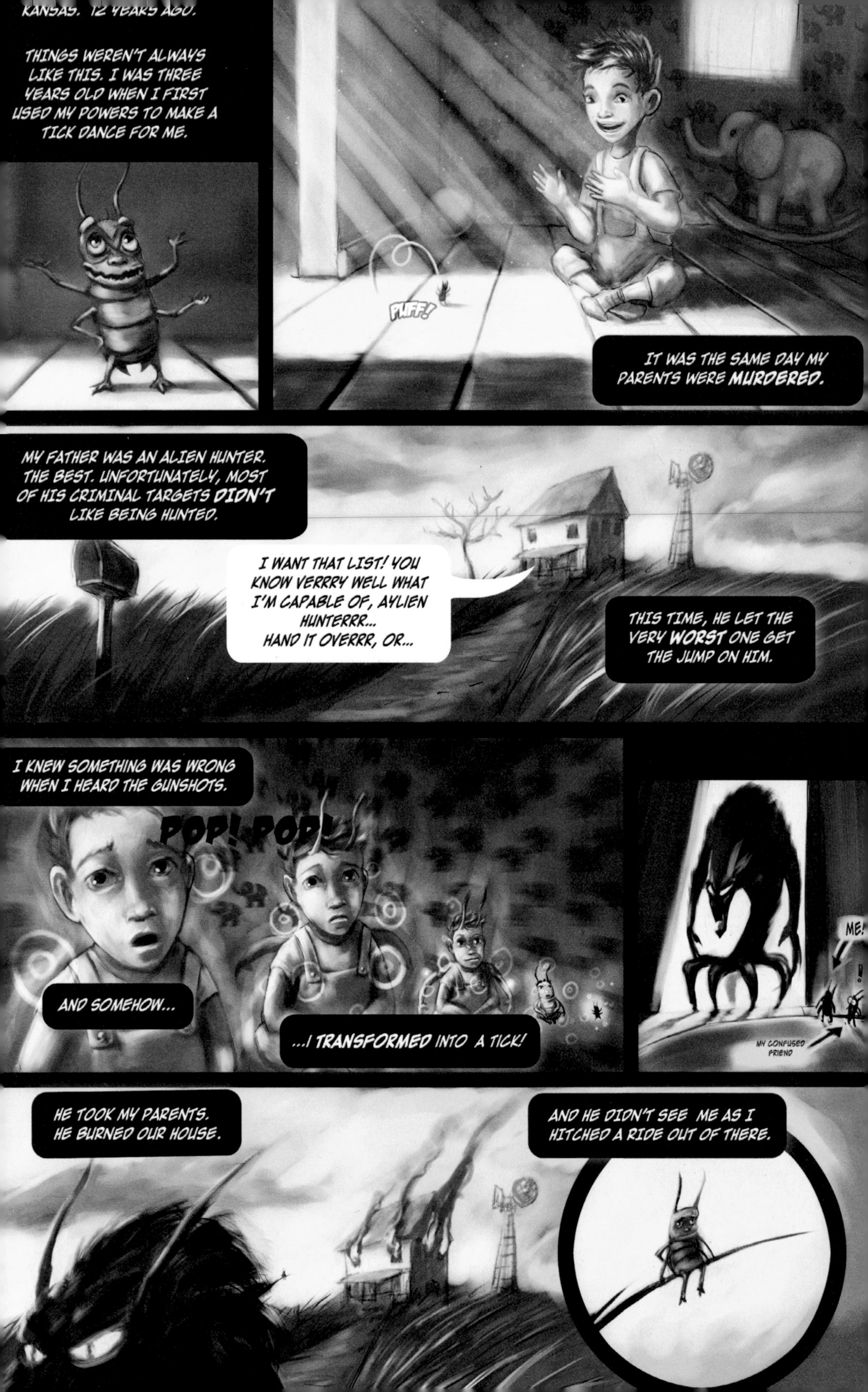
KANSAS. 12 YEARS AGO.
THINGS WEREN'T ALWAYS LIKE THIS. I WAS THREE YEARS OLD WHEN I FIRST USED MY POWERS TO MAKE A TICK DANCE FOR ME.
PUFF!
IT WAS THE SAME DAY MY PARENTS WERE MURDERED.
MY FATHER WAS AN ALIEN HUNTER. THE BEST. UNFORTUNATELY, MOST OF HIS CRIMINAL TARGETS DIDN'T LIKE BEING HUNTED.
I WANT THAT LIST! YOU KNOW VERRRY WELL WHAT I'M CAPABLE OF, AYLIEN HUNTERRR... HAND IT OVERRR, OR...
THIS TIME, HE LET THE VERY WORST ONE GET THE JUMP ON HIM.
I KNEW SOMETHING WAS WRONG WHEN I HEARD THE GUNSHOTS.
POP! POP!
AND SOMEHOW...
...I TRANSFORMED INTO A TICK!
ME!
!
MY CONFUSED FRIEND
HE TOOK MY PARENTS. HE BURNED OUR HOUSE.
AND HE DIDN'T SEE ME AS I HITCHED A RIDE OUT OF THERE.

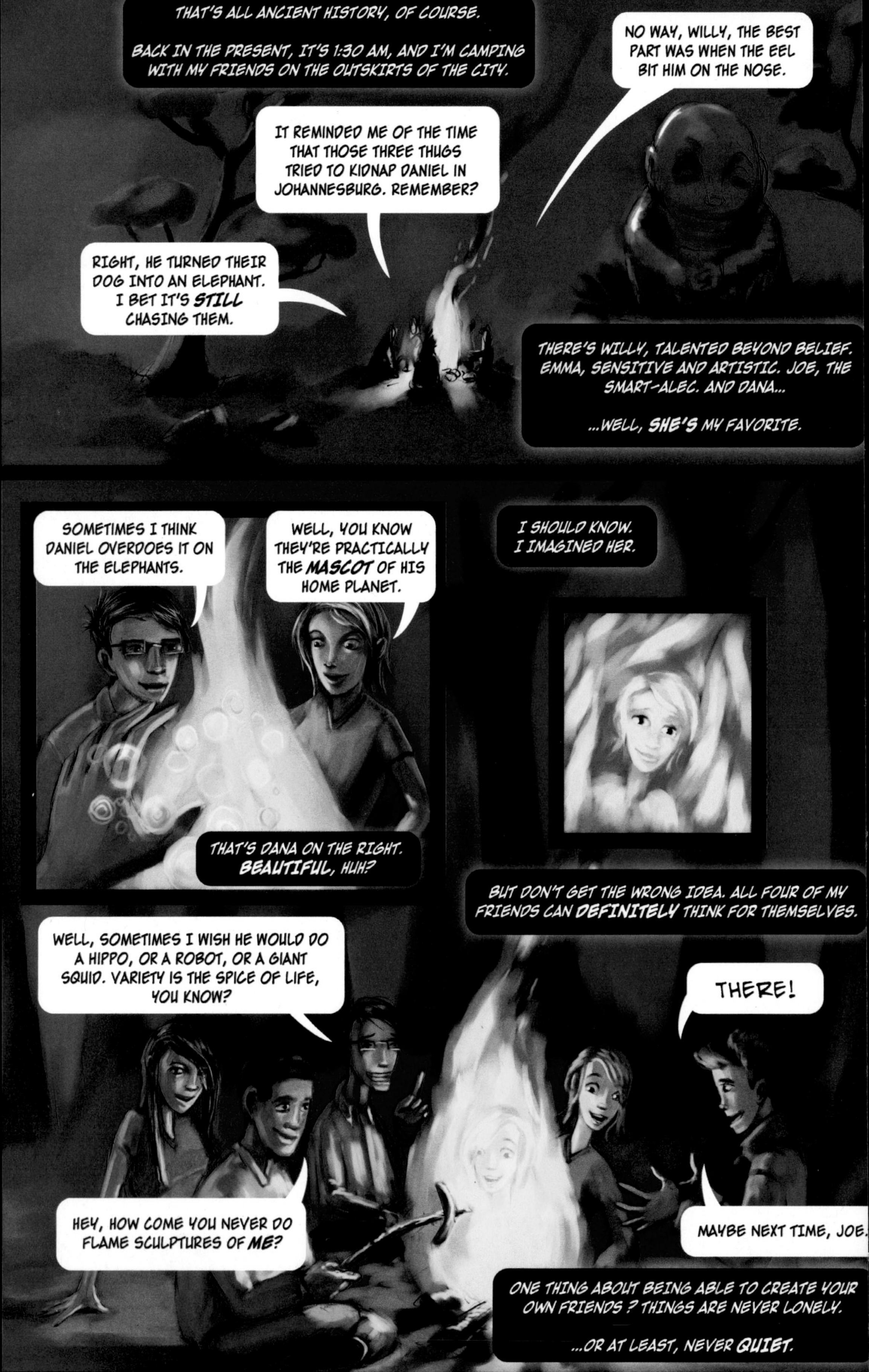
THAT'S ALL ANCIENT HISTORY, OF COURSE.
BACK IN THE PRESENT, IT'S 1:30 AM, AND I'M CAMPING WITH MY FRIENDS ON THE OUTSKIRTS OF THE CITY.
NO WAY, WILLY, THE BEST PART WAS WHEN THE EEL BIT HIM ON THE NOSE.
IT REMINDED ME OF THE TIME THAT THOSE THREE THUGS TRIED TO KIDNAP DANIEL IN JOHANNESBURG. REMEMBER?
RIGHT, HE TURNED THEIR DOG INTO AN ELEPHANT. I BET IT'S STILL CHASING THEM.
THERE'S WILLY, TALENTED BEYOND BELIEF. EMMA, SENSITIVE AND ARTISTIC. JOE, THE SMART-ALEC. AND DANA...
...WELL, SHE'S MY FAVORITE.
SOMETIMES I THINK DANIEL OVERDOES IT ON THE ELEPHANTS.
WELL, YOU KNOW THEY'RE PRACTICALLY THE MASCOT OF HIS HOME PLANET.
THAT'S DANA ON THE RIGHT. BEAUTIFUL, HUH?
I SHOULD KNOW. I IMAGINED HER.
BUT DON'T GET THE WRONG IDEA. ALL FOUR OF MY FRIENDS CAN DEFINITELY THINK FOR THEMSELVES.
WELL, SOMETIMES I WISH HE WOULD DO A HIPPO, OR A ROBOT, OR A GIANT SQUID. VARIETY IS THE SPICE OF LIFE, YOU KNOW?
THERE!
HEY, HOW COME YOU NEVER DO FLAME SCULPTURES OF ME?
MAYBE NEXT TIME, JOE.
ONE THING ABOUT BEING ABLE TO CREATE YOUR OWN FRIENDS ? THINGS ARE NEVER LONELY.
...OR AT LEAST, NEVER QUIET.

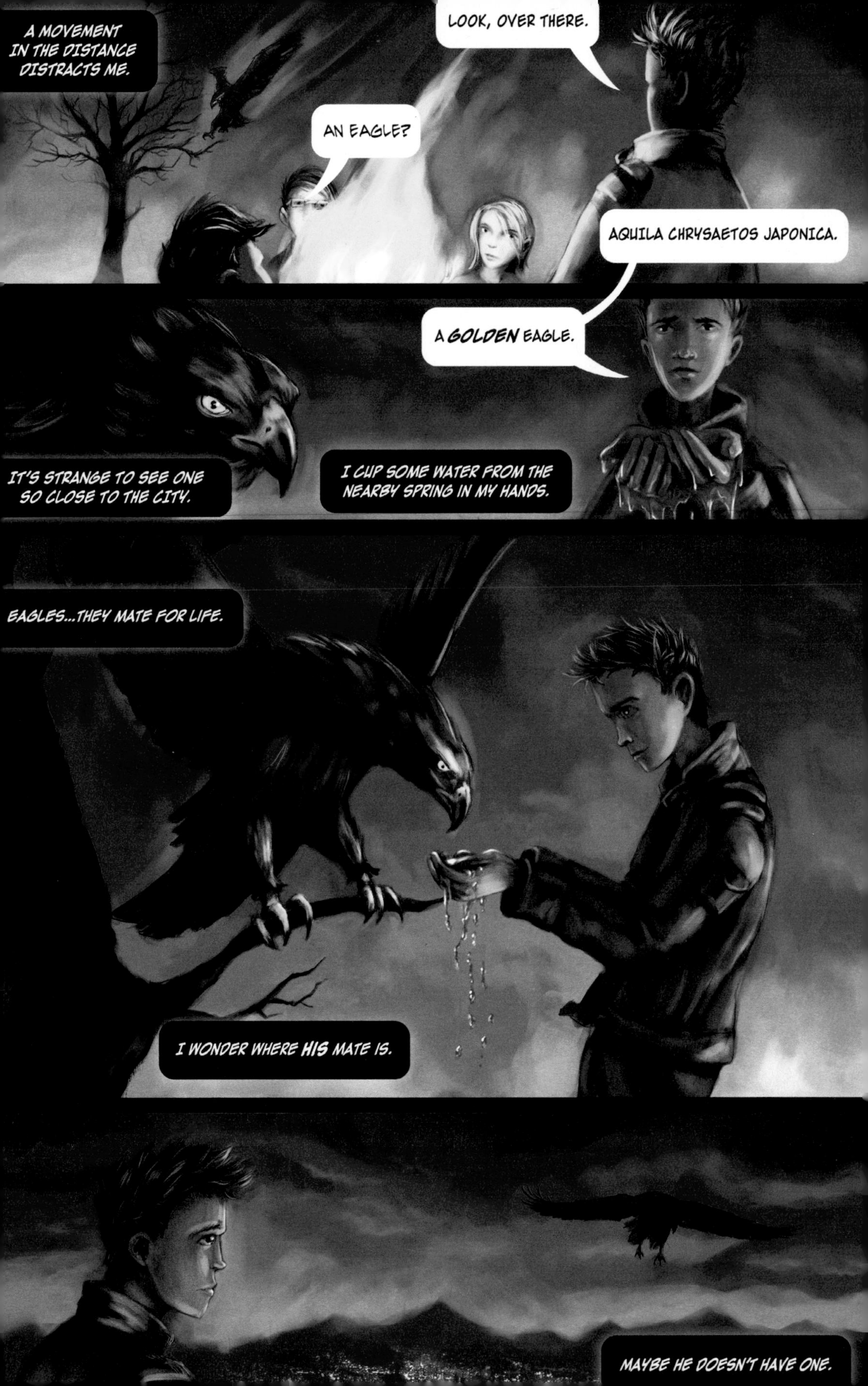
A MOVEMENT IN THE DISTANCE DISTRACTS ME.
LOOK, OVER THERE.
AN EAGLE?
AQUILA CHRYSAETOS JAPONICA.
A **GOLDEN** EAGLE.
IT'S STRANGE TO SEE ONE SO CLOSE TO THE CITY.
I CUP SOME WATER FROM THE NEARBY SPRING IN MY HANDS.
EAGLES...THEY MATE FOR LIFE.
I WONDER WHERE **HIS** MATE IS.
MAYBE HE DOESN'T HAVE ONE.

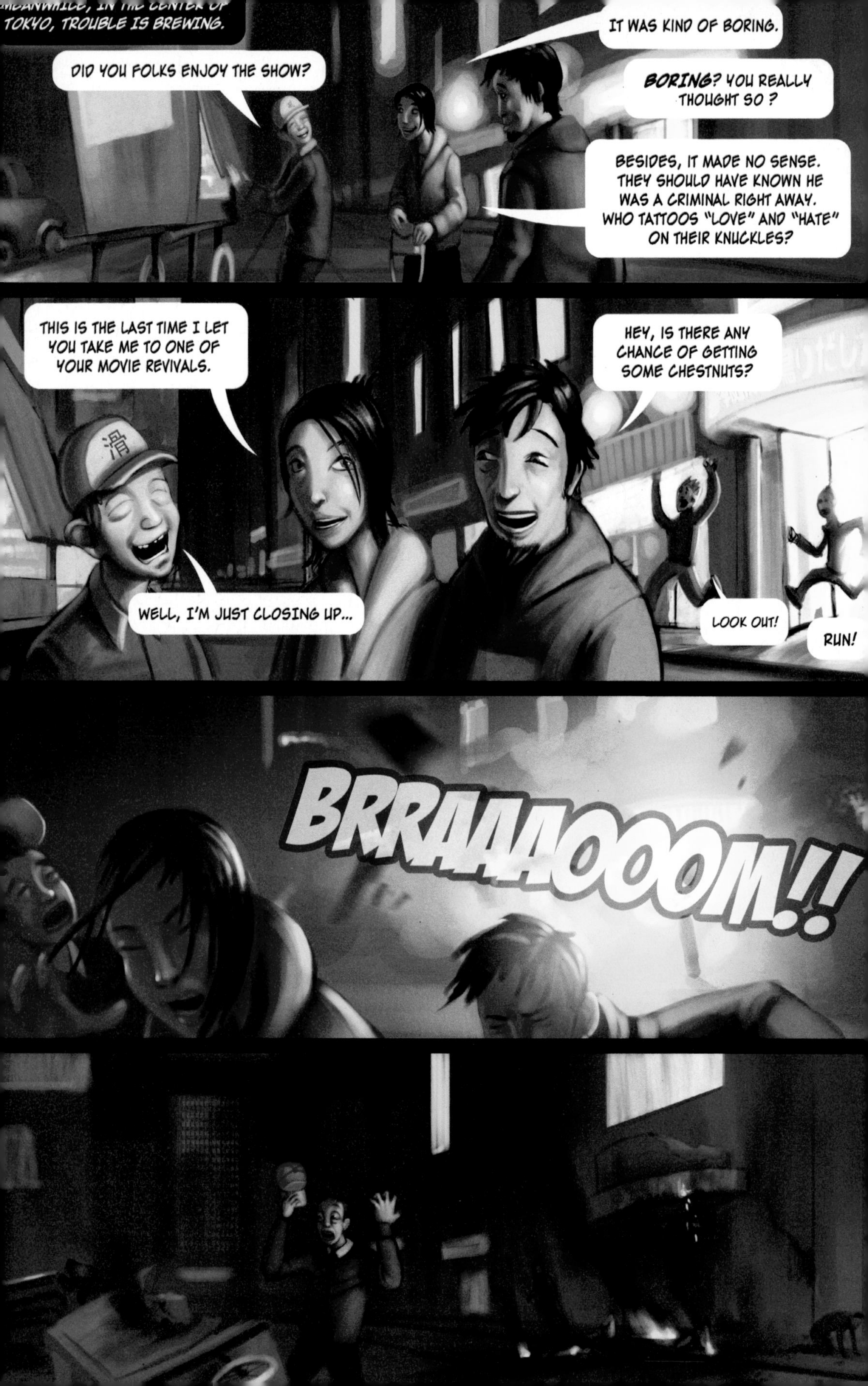
TOKYO, TROUBLE IS BREWING.
DID YOU FOLKS ENJOY THE SHOW?
IT WAS KIND OF BORING.
BORING? YOU REALLY THOUGHT SO ?
BESIDES, IT MADE NO SENSE. THEY SHOULD HAVE KNOWN HE WAS A CRIMINAL RIGHT AWAY. WHO TATTOOS "LOVE" AND "HATE" ON THEIR KNUCKLES?
THIS IS THE LAST TIME I LET YOU TAKE ME TO ONE OF YOUR MOVIE REVIVALS.
HEY, IS THERE ANY CHANCE OF GETTING SOME CHESTNUTS?
WELL, I'M JUST CLOSING UP...
LOOK OUT!
RUN!
BRRAAAOOOM!!

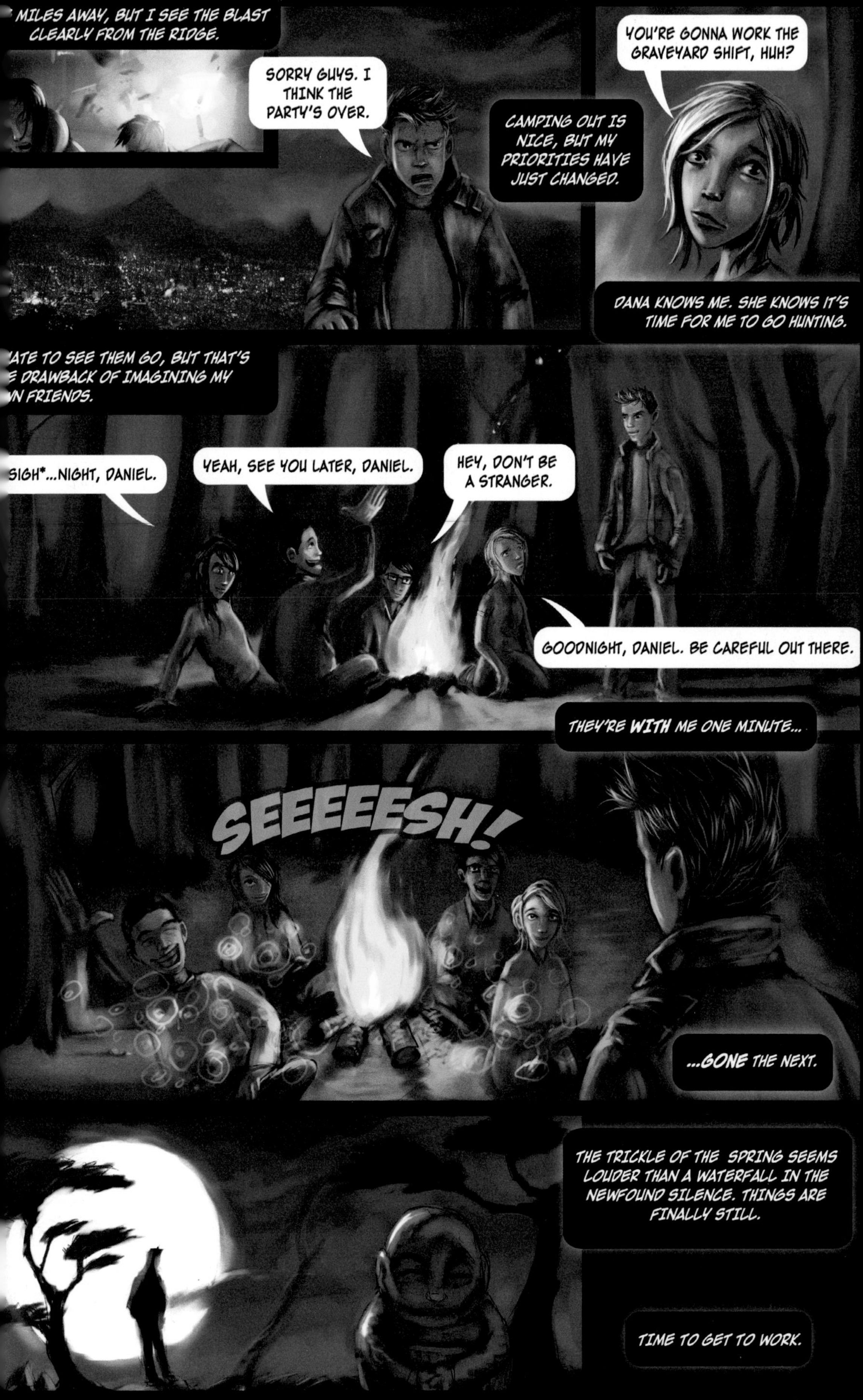

MILES AWAY, BUT I SEE THE BLAST CLEARLY FROM THE RIDGE.
SORRY GUYS. I THINK THE PARTY'S OVER.
CAMPING OUT IS NICE, BUT MY PRIORITIES HAVE JUST CHANGED.
YOU'RE GONNA WORK THE GRAVEYARD SHIFT, HUH?
DANA KNOWS ME. SHE KNOWS IT'S TIME FOR ME TO GO HUNTING.
ATE TO SEE THEM GO, BUT THAT'S E DRAWBACK OF IMAGINING MY N FRIENDS.
SIGH*...NIGHT, DANIEL.
YEAH, SEE YOU LATER, DANIEL.
HEY, DON'T BE A STRANGER.
GOODNIGHT, DANIEL. BE CAREFUL OUT THERE.
THEY'RE **WITH** ME ONE MINUTE...
SEEEEEESH!
...**GONE** THE NEXT.
THE TRICKLE OF THE SPRING SEEMS LOUDER THAN A WATERFALL IN THE NEWFOUND SILENCE. THINGS ARE FINALLY STILL.
TIME TO GET TO WORK.

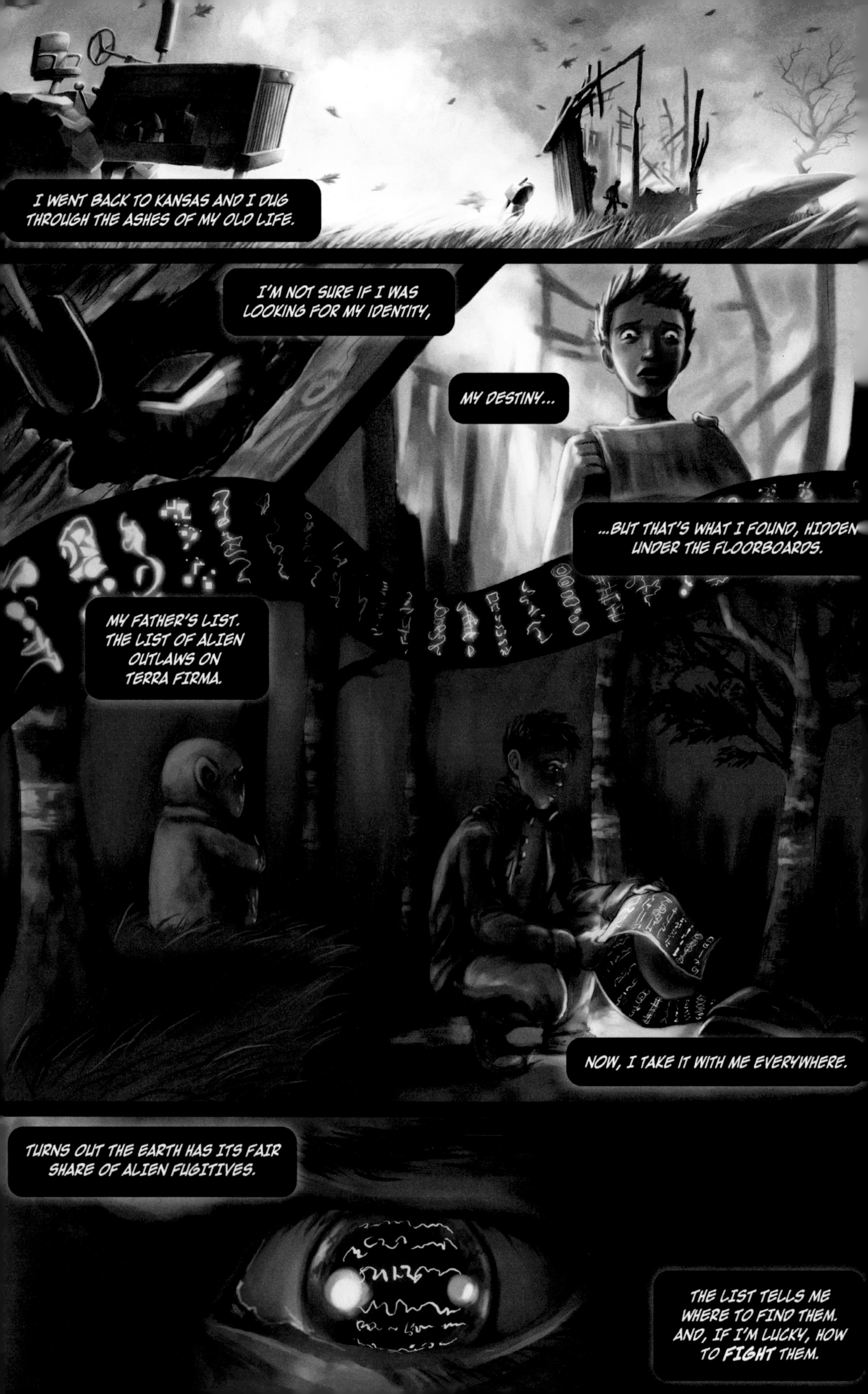
I WENT BACK TO KANSAS AND I DUG THROUGH THE ASHES OF MY OLD LIFE.
I'M NOT SURE IF I WAS LOOKING FOR MY IDENTITY,
MY DESTINY...
...BUT THAT'S WHAT I FOUND, HIDDEN UNDER THE FLOORBOARDS.
MY FATHER'S LIST. THE LIST OF ALIEN OUTLAWS ON TERRA FIRMA.
NOW, I TAKE IT WITH ME EVERYWHERE.
TURNS OUT THE EARTH HAS ITS FAIR SHARE OF ALIEN FUGITIVES.
THE LIST TELLS ME WHERE TO FIND THEM. AND, IF I'M LUCKY, HOW TO FIGHT THEM.

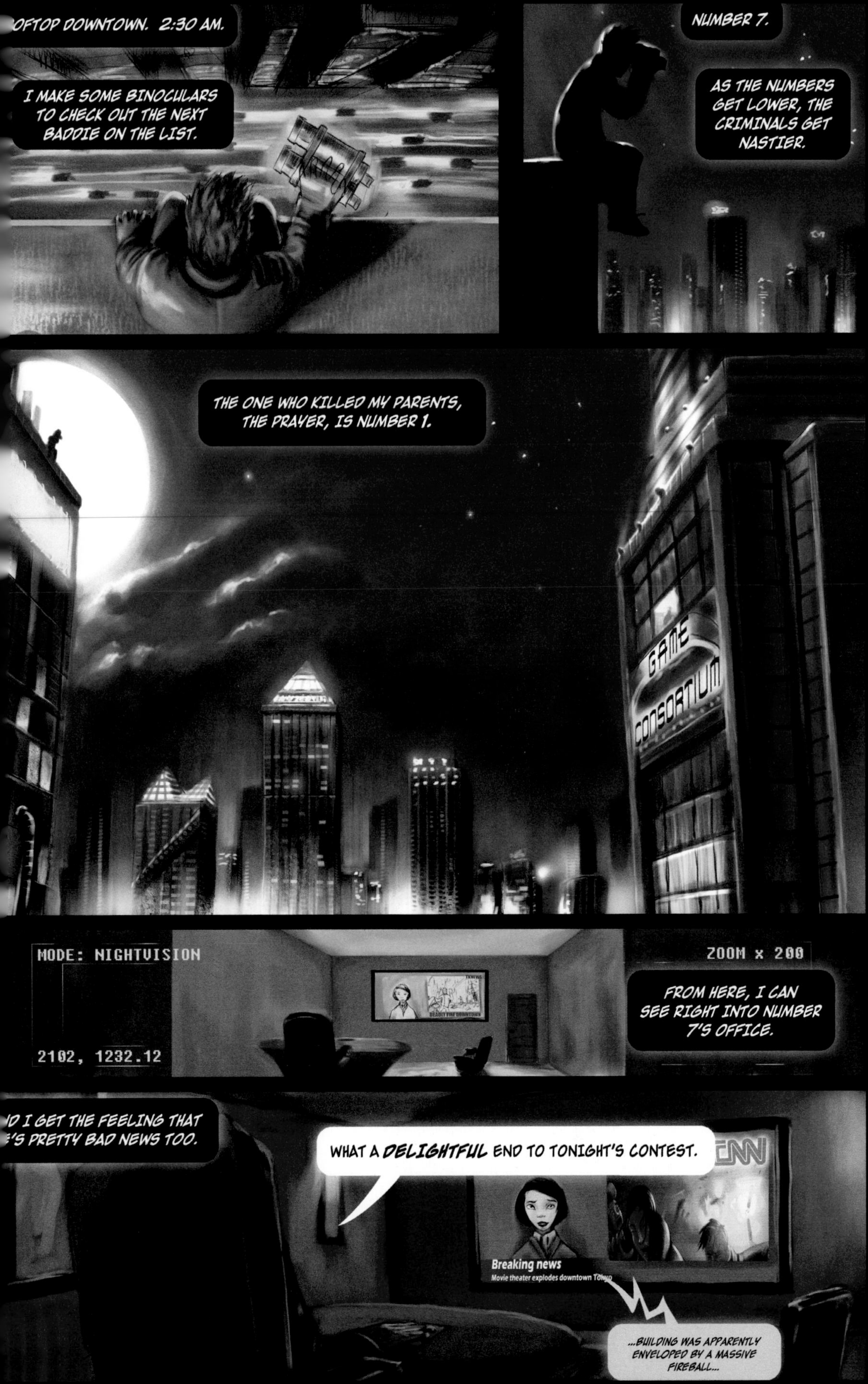
OFTOP DOWNTOWN. 2:30 AM.
I MAKE SOME BINOCULARS TO CHECK OUT THE NEXT BADDIE ON THE LIST.
NUMBER 7.
AS THE NUMBERS GET LOWER, THE CRIMINALS GET NASTIER.
THE ONE WHO KILLED MY PARENTS, THE PRAYER, IS NUMBER 1.
GAME CONSORTIUM
MODE: NIGHTVISION
2102, 1232.12
ZOOM x 200
FROM HERE, I CAN SEE RIGHT INTO NUMBER 7'S OFFICE.
ID I GET THE FEELING THAT 'S PRETTY BAD NEWS TOO.
WHAT A DELIGHTFUL END TO TONIGHT'S CONTEST.
Breaking news
Movie theater explodes downtown Tokyo
...BUILDING WAS APPARENTLY ENVELOPED BY A MASSIVE FIREBALL...

CHAPTER 2
FATHER AND SONS

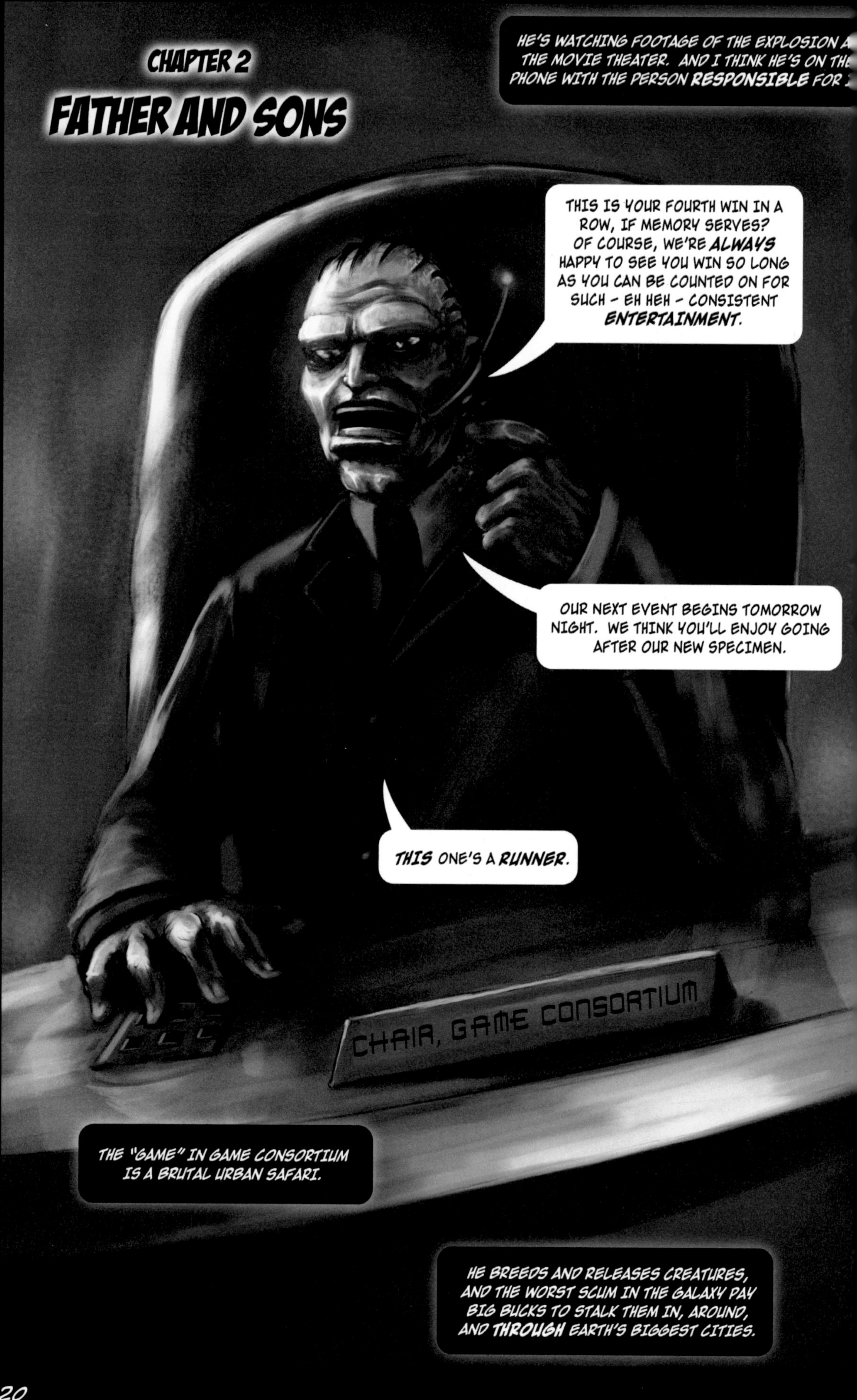
HE'S WATCHING FOOTAGE OF THE EXPLOSION A
THE MOVIE THEATER. AND I THINK HE'S ON TH
PHONE WITH THE PERSON **RESPONSIBLE** FOR
THIS IS YOUR FOURTH WIN IN A ROW, IF MEMORY SERVES? OF COURSE, WE'RE **ALWAYS** HAPPY TO SEE YOU WIN SO LONG AS YOU CAN BE COUNTED ON FOR SUCH - EH HEH - CONSISTENT **ENTERTAINMENT**.
OUR NEXT EVENT BEGINS TOMORROW NIGHT. WE THINK YOU'LL ENJOY GOING AFTER OUR NEW SPECIMEN.
THIS ONE'S A **RUNNER**.
CHAIR, GAME CONSORTIUM
THE "GAME" IN GAME CONSORTIUM IS A BRUTAL URBAN SAFARI.
HE BREEDS AND RELEASES CREATURES, AND THE WORST SCUM IN THE GALAXY PAY BIG BUCKS TO STALK THEM IN, AROUND, AND **THROUGH** EARTH'S BIGGEST CITIES.

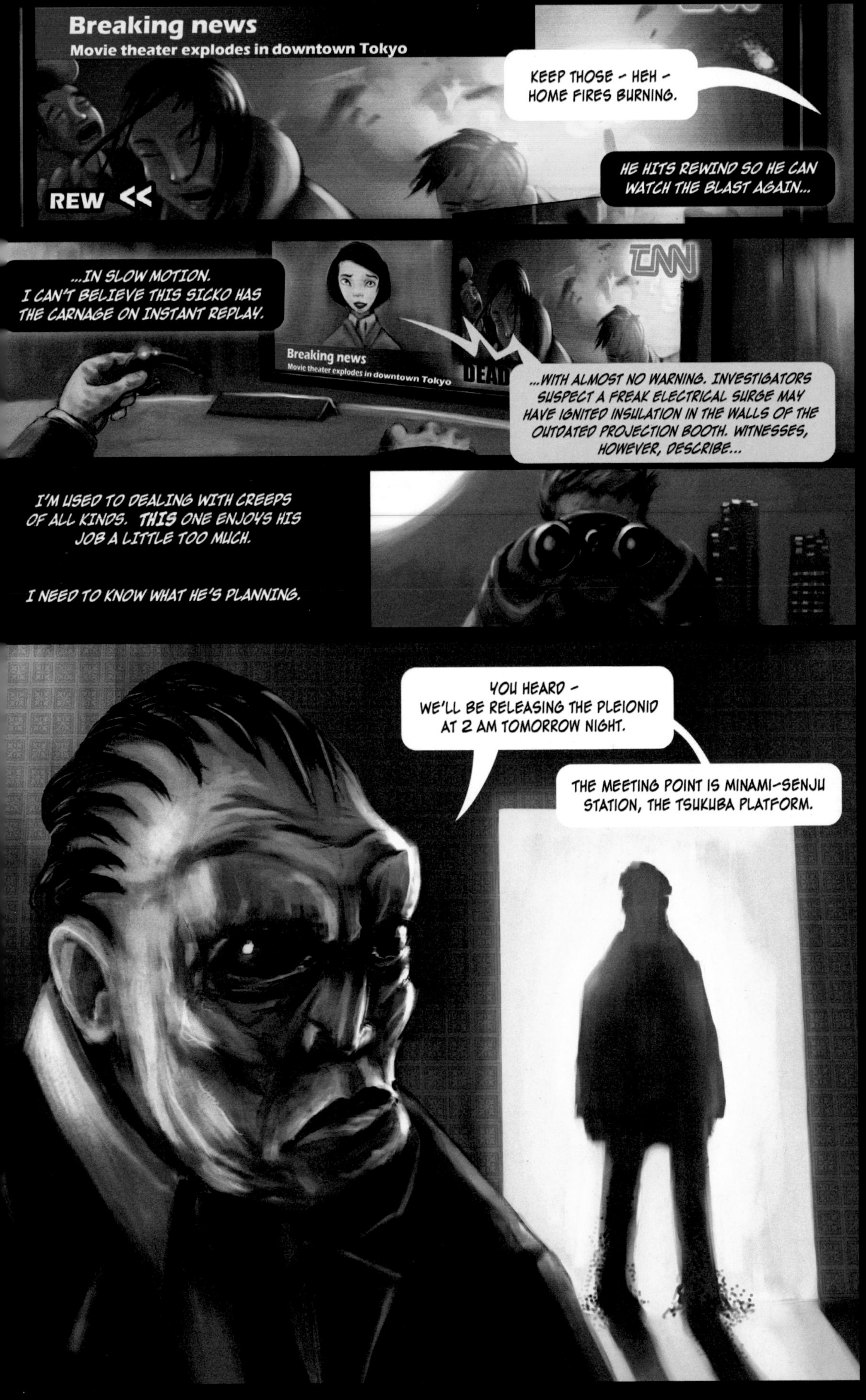
Breaking news
Movie theater explodes in downtown Tokyo
KEEP THOSE - HEH - HOME FIRES BURNING.
REW <<
HE HITS REWIND SO HE CAN WATCH THE BLAST AGAIN...
...IN SLOW MOTION. I CAN'T BELIEVE THIS SICKO HAS THE CARNAGE ON INSTANT REPLAY.
Breaking news
Movie theater explodes in downtown Tokyo
TNN
...WITH ALMOST NO WARNING. INVESTIGATORS SUSPECT A FREAK ELECTRICAL SURGE MAY HAVE IGNITED INSULATION IN THE WALLS OF THE OUTDATED PROJECTION BOOTH. WITNESSES, HOWEVER, DESCRIBE...
I'M USED TO DEALING WITH CREEPS OF ALL KINDS. THIS ONE ENJOYS HIS JOB A LITTLE TOO MUCH.
I NEED TO KNOW WHAT HE'S PLANNING.
YOU HEARD - WE'LL BE RELEASING THE PLEIONID AT 2 AM TOMORROW NIGHT.
THE MEETING POINT IS MINAMI-SENJU STATION, THE TSUKUBA PLATFORM.

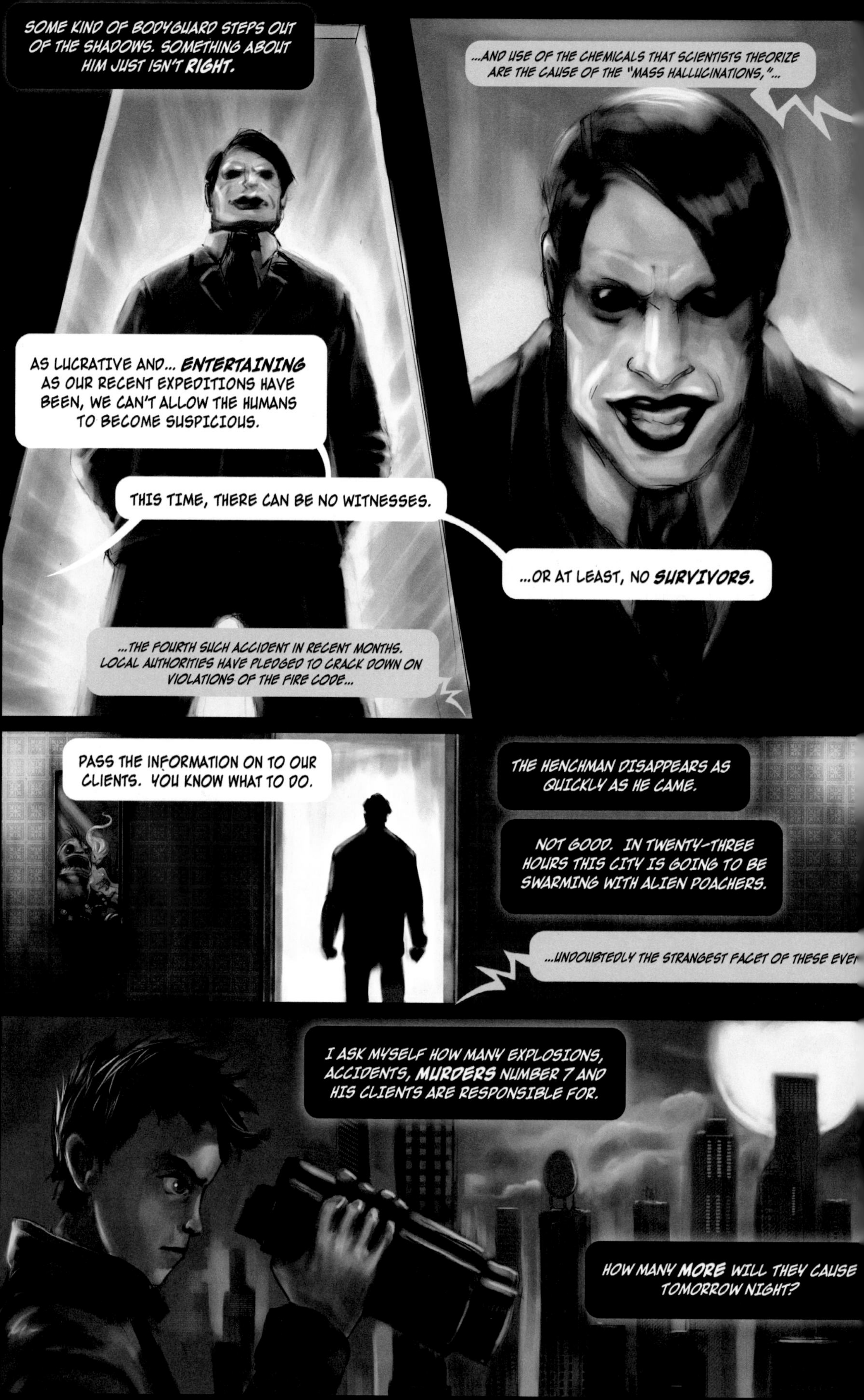
SOME KIND OF BODYGUARD STEPS OUT OF THE SHADOWS. SOMETHING ABOUT HIM JUST ISN'T RIGHT.
...AND USE OF THE CHEMICALS THAT SCIENTISTS THEORIZE ARE THE CAUSE OF THE "MASS HALLUCINATIONS,"...
AS LUCRATIVE AND... ENTERTAINING AS OUR RECENT EXPEDITIONS HAVE BEEN, WE CAN'T ALLOW THE HUMANS TO BECOME SUSPICIOUS.
THIS TIME, THERE CAN BE NO WITNESSES.
...OR AT LEAST, NO SURVIVORS.
...THE FOURTH SUCH ACCIDENT IN RECENT MONTHS. LOCAL AUTHORITIES HAVE PLEDGED TO CRACK DOWN ON VIOLATIONS OF THE FIRE CODE...
PASS THE INFORMATION ON TO OUR CLIENTS. YOU KNOW WHAT TO DO.
THE HENCHMAN DISAPPEARS AS QUICKLY AS HE CAME.
NOT GOOD. IN TWENTY-THREE HOURS THIS CITY IS GOING TO BE SWARMING WITH ALIEN POACHERS.
...UNDOUBTEDLY THE STRANGEST FACET OF THESE EVE
I ASK MYSELF HOW MANY EXPLOSIONS, ACCIDENTS, MURDERS NUMBER 7 AND HIS CLIENTS ARE RESPONSIBLE FOR.
HOW MANY MORE WILL THEY CAUSE TOMORROW NIGHT?

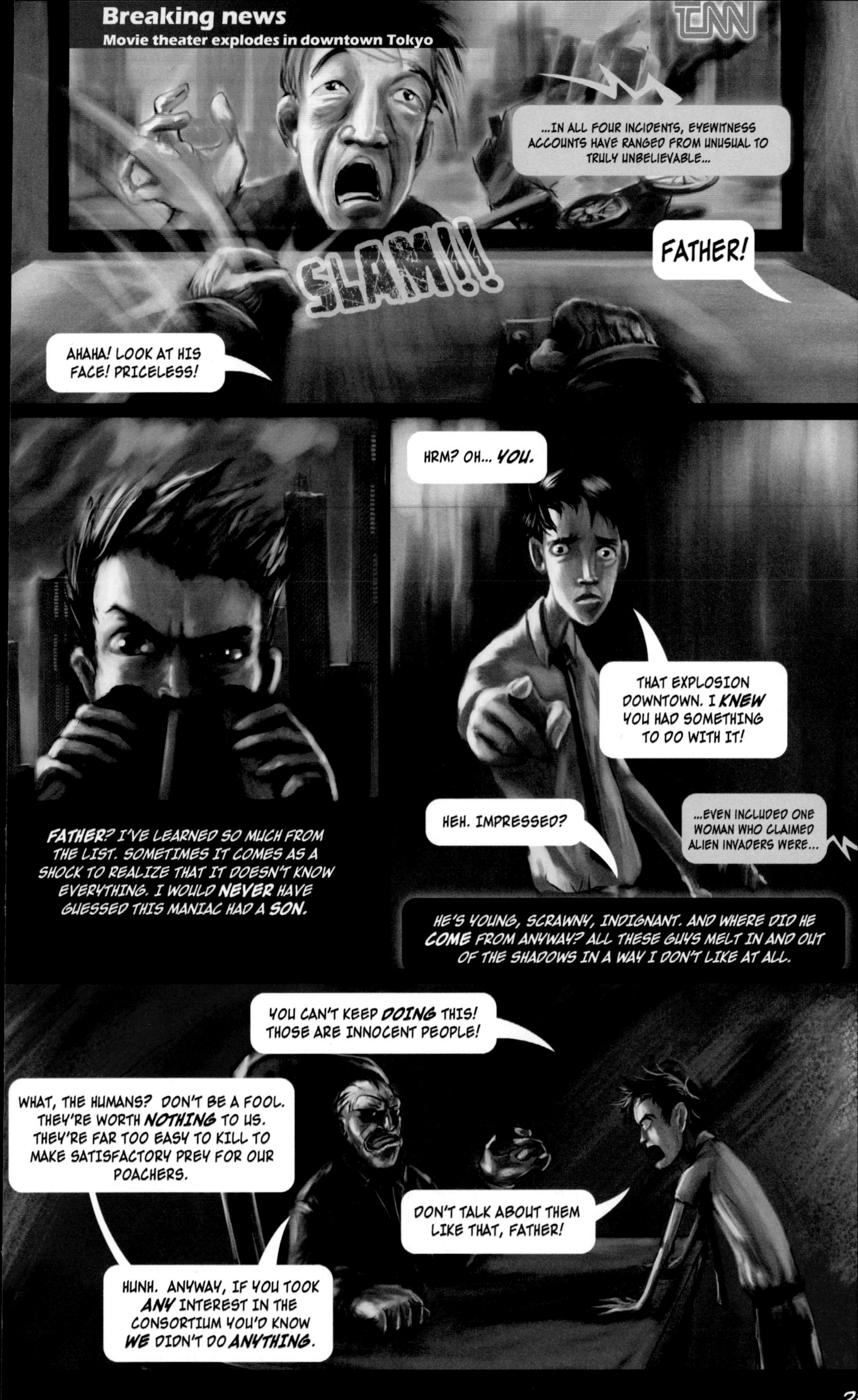
Breaking news
Movie theater explodes in downtown Tokyo
TNN
...IN ALL FOUR INCIDENTS, EYEWITNESS ACCOUNTS HAVE RANGED FROM UNUSUAL TO TRULY UNBELIEVABLE...
FATHER!
SLAM!!
AHAHA! LOOK AT HIS FACE! PRICELESS!
HRM? OH... YOU.
THAT EXPLOSION DOWNTOWN. I KNEW YOU HAD SOMETHING TO DO WITH IT!
FATHER? I'VE LEARNED SO MUCH FROM THE LIST. SOMETIMES IT COMES AS A SHOCK TO REALIZE THAT IT DOESN'T KNOW EVERYTHING. I WOULD NEVER HAVE GUESSED THIS MANIAC HAD A SON.
HEH. IMPRESSED?
...EVEN INCLUDED ONE WOMAN WHO CLAIMED ALIEN INVADERS WERE...
HE'S YOUNG, SCRAWNY, INDIGNANT. AND WHERE DID HE COME FROM ANYWAY? ALL THESE GUYS MELT IN AND OUT OF THE SHADOWS IN A WAY I DON'T LIKE AT ALL.
YOU CAN'T KEEP DOING THIS! THOSE ARE INNOCENT PEOPLE!
WHAT, THE HUMANS? DON'T BE A FOOL. THEY'RE WORTH NOTHING TO US. THEY'RE FAR TOO EASY TO KILL TO MAKE SATISFACTORY PREY FOR OUR POACHERS.
DON'T TALK ABOUT THEM LIKE THAT, FATHER!
HUNH. ANYWAY, IF YOU TOOK ANY INTEREST IN THE CONSORTIUM YOU'D KNOW WE DIDN'T DO ANYTHING.

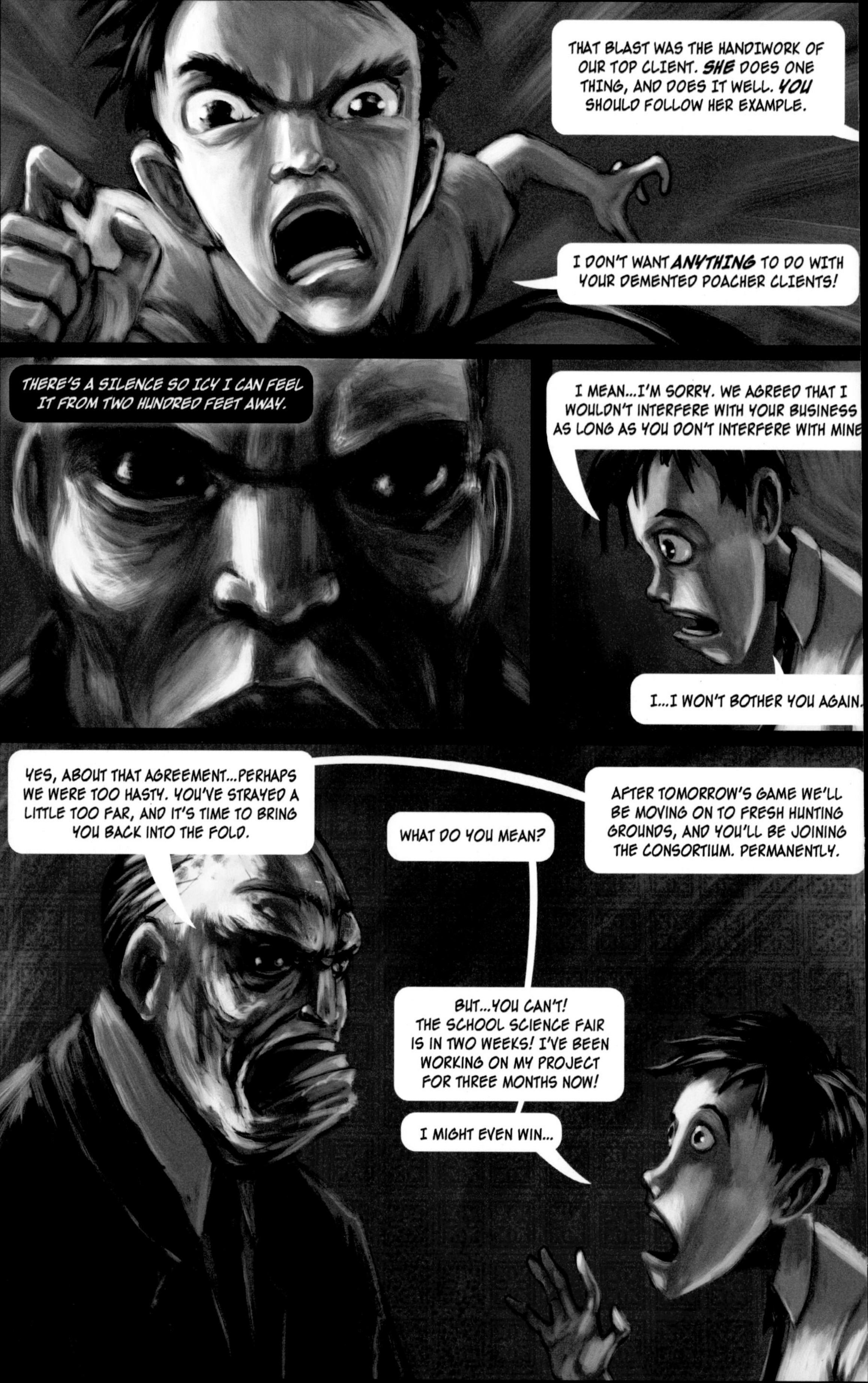
THAT BLAST WAS THE HANDIWORK OF OUR TOP CLIENT. SHE DOES ONE THING, AND DOES IT WELL. YOU SHOULD FOLLOW HER EXAMPLE.
I DON'T WANT ANYTHING TO DO WITH YOUR DEMENTED POACHER CLIENTS!
THERE'S A SILENCE SO ICY I CAN FEEL IT FROM TWO HUNDRED FEET AWAY.
I MEAN...I'M SORRY. WE AGREED THAT I WOULDN'T INTERFERE WITH YOUR BUSINESS AS LONG AS YOU DON'T INTERFERE WITH MINE
I...I WON'T BOTHER YOU AGAIN.
YES, ABOUT THAT AGREEMENT...PERHAPS WE WERE TOO HASTY. YOU'VE STRAYED A LITTLE TOO FAR, AND IT'S TIME TO BRING YOU BACK INTO THE FOLD.
WHAT DO YOU MEAN?
AFTER TOMORROW'S GAME WE'LL BE MOVING ON TO FRESH HUNTING GROUNDS, AND YOU'LL BE JOINING THE CONSORTIUM. PERMANENTLY.
BUT...YOU CAN'T! THE SCHOOL SCIENCE FAIR IS IN TWO WEEKS! I'VE BEEN WORKING ON MY PROJECT FOR THREE MONTHS NOW!
I MIGHT EVEN WIN...

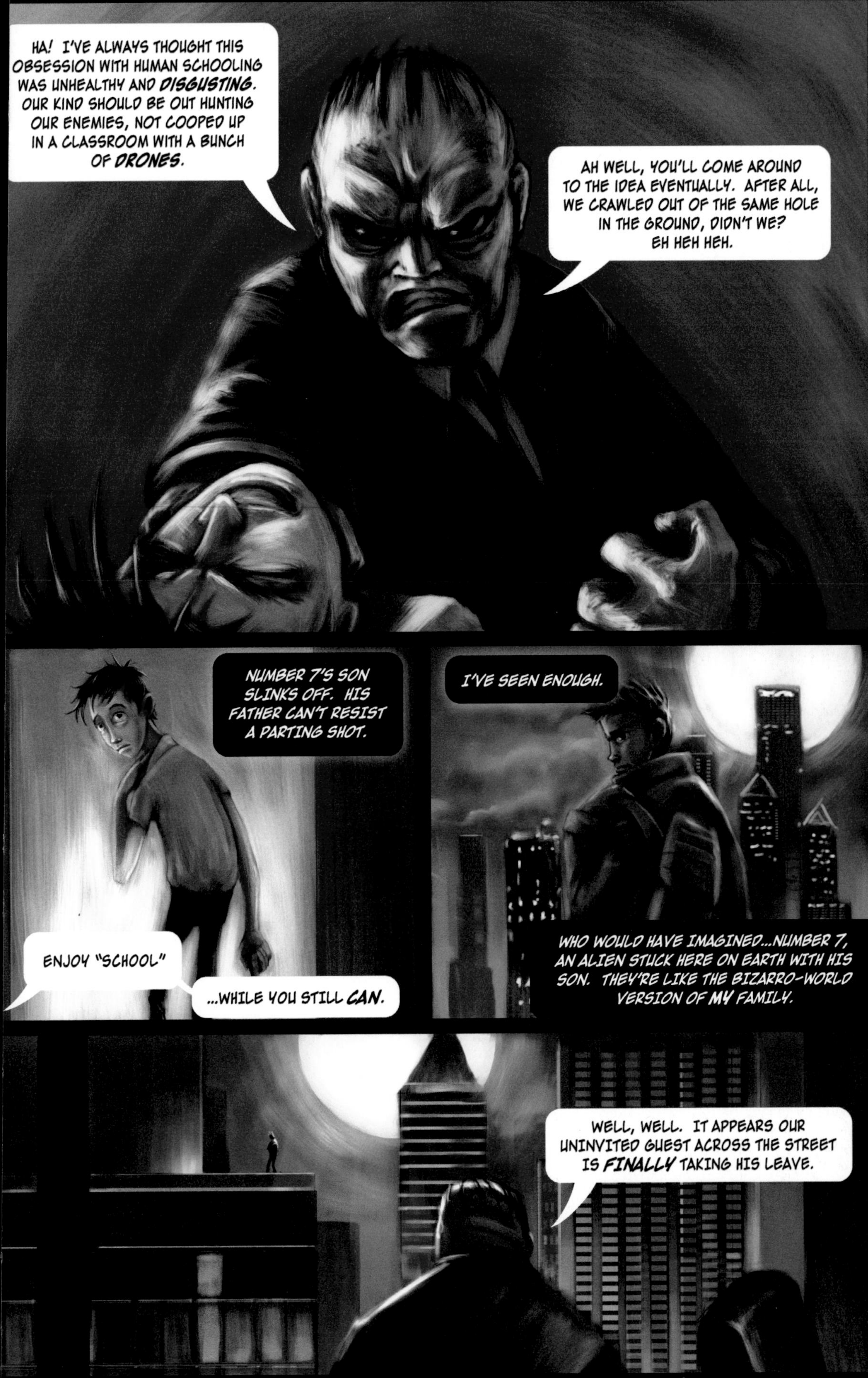
HA! I'VE ALWAYS THOUGHT THIS OBSESSION WITH HUMAN SCHOOLING WAS UNHEALTHY AND DISGUSTING. OUR KIND SHOULD BE OUT HUNTING OUR ENEMIES, NOT COOPED UP IN A CLASSROOM WITH A BUNCH OF DRONES.
AH WELL, YOU'LL COME AROUND TO THE IDEA EVENTUALLY. AFTER ALL, WE CRAWLED OUT OF THE SAME HOLE IN THE GROUND, DIDN'T WE? EH HEH HEH.
NUMBER 7'S SON SLINKS OFF. HIS FATHER CAN'T RESIST A PARTING SHOT.
ENJOY "SCHOOL"
...WHILE YOU STILL CAN.
I'VE SEEN ENOUGH.
WHO WOULD HAVE IMAGINED...NUMBER 7, AN ALIEN STUCK HERE ON EARTH WITH HIS SON. THEY'RE LIKE THE BIZARRO-WORLD VERSION OF MY FAMILY.
WELL, WELL. IT APPEARS OUR UNINVITED GUEST ACROSS THE STREET IS FINALLY TAKING HIS LEAVE.

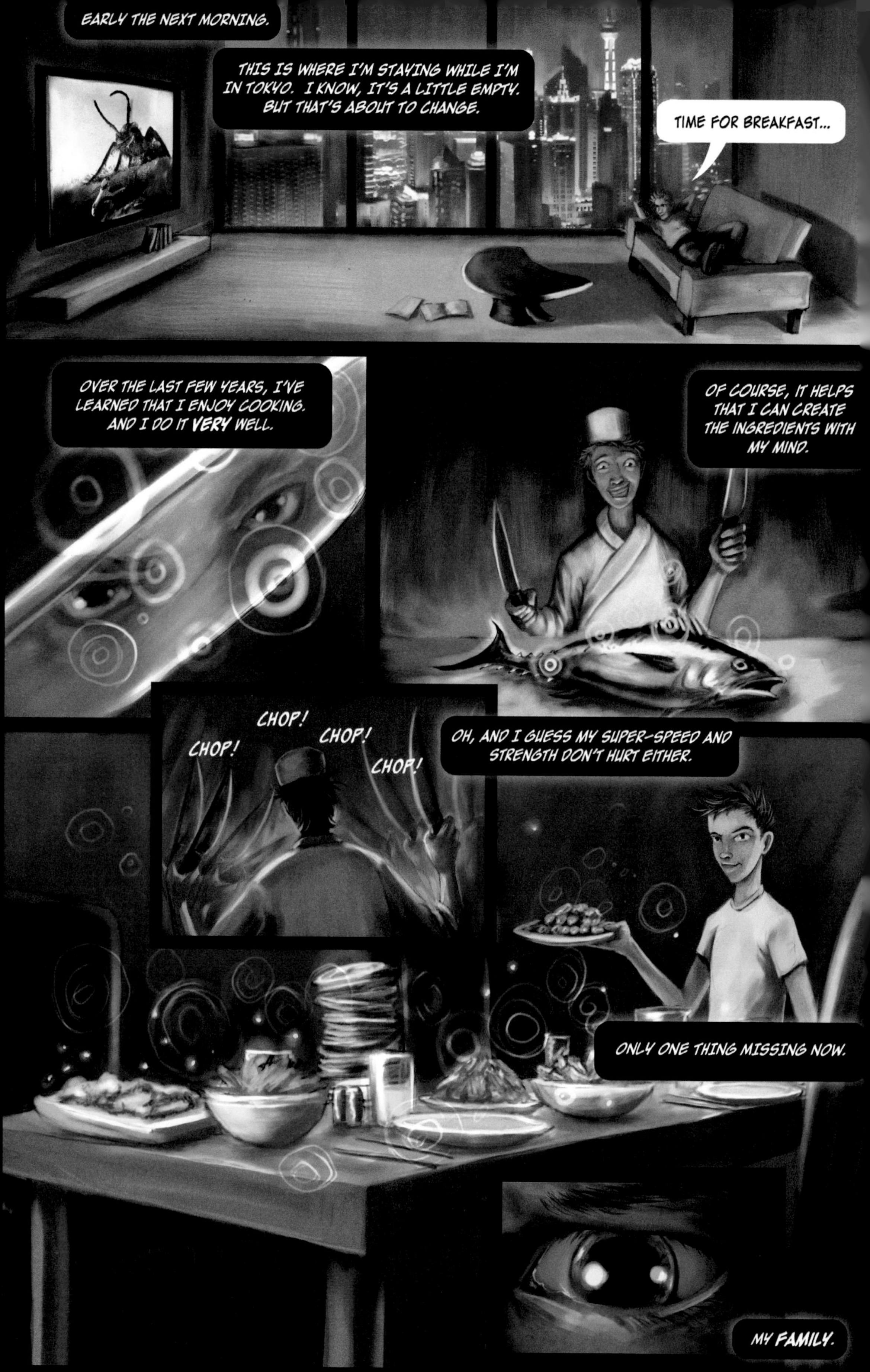
EARLY THE NEXT MORNING.
THIS IS WHERE I'M STAYING WHILE I'M IN TOKYO. I KNOW, IT'S A LITTLE EMPTY. BUT THAT'S ABOUT TO CHANGE.
TIME FOR BREAKFAST...
OVER THE LAST FEW YEARS, I'VE LEARNED THAT I ENJOY COOKING. AND I DO IT VERY WELL.
OF COURSE, IT HELPS THAT I CAN CREATE THE INGREDIENTS WITH MY MIND.
CHOP!
CHOP!
CHOP!
CHOP!
OH, AND I GUESS MY SUPER-SPEED AND STRENGTH DON'T HURT EITHER.
ONLY ONE THING MISSING NOW.
MY FAMILY.

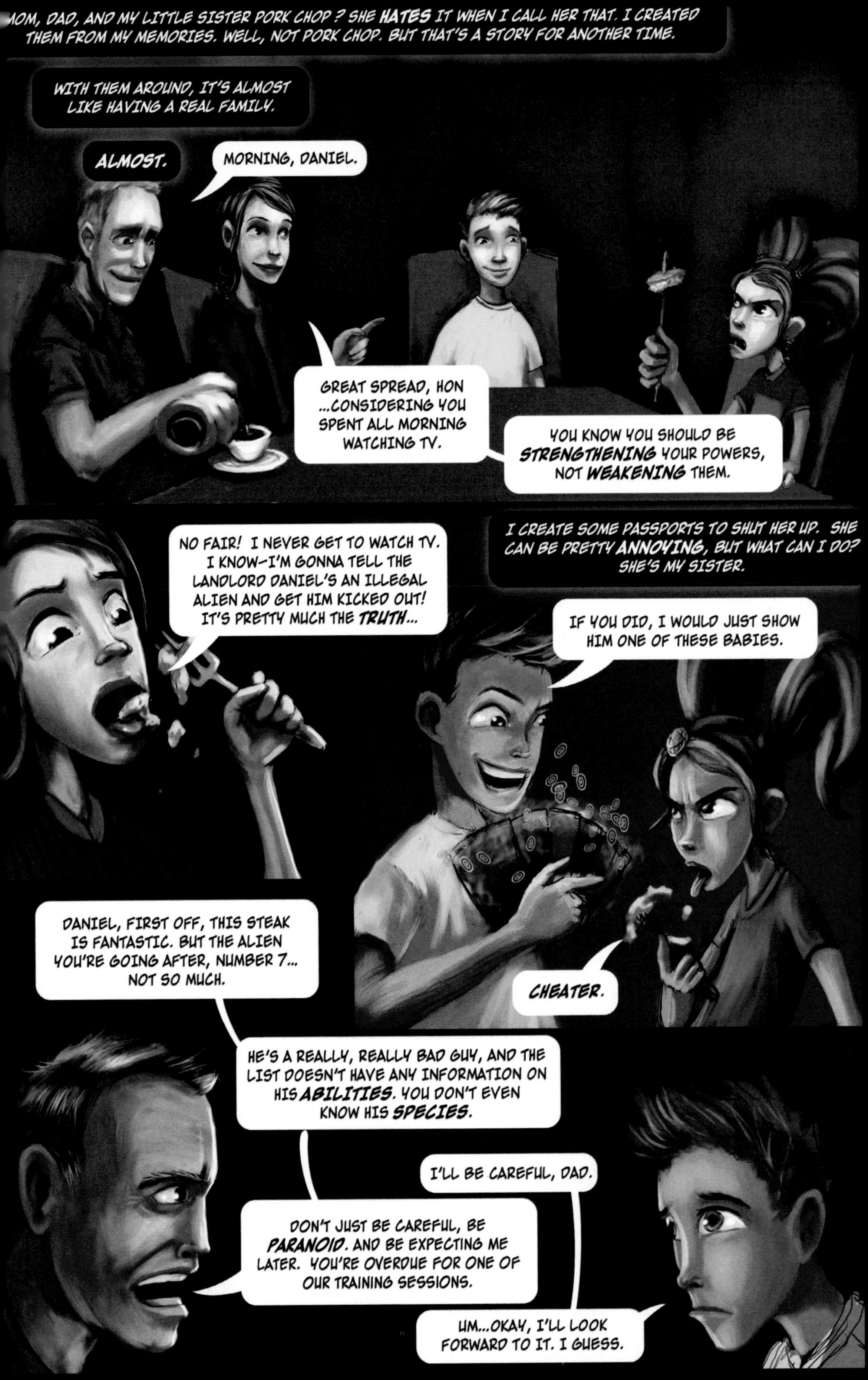
MOM, DAD, AND MY LITTLE SISTER PORK CHOP? SHE HATES IT WHEN I CALL HER THAT. I CREATED THEM FROM MY MEMORIES. WELL, NOT PORK CHOP. BUT THAT'S A STORY FOR ANOTHER TIME.
WITH THEM AROUND, IT'S ALMOST LIKE HAVING A REAL FAMILY.
ALMOST.
MORNING, DANIEL.
GREAT SPREAD, HON ...CONSIDERING YOU SPENT ALL MORNING WATCHING TV.
YOU KNOW YOU SHOULD BE STRENGTHENING YOUR POWERS, NOT WEAKENING THEM.
NO FAIR! I NEVER GET TO WATCH TV. I KNOW—I'M GONNA TELL THE LANDLORD DANIEL'S AN ILLEGAL ALIEN AND GET HIM KICKED OUT! IT'S PRETTY MUCH THE TRUTH...
I CREATE SOME PASSPORTS TO SHUT HER UP. SHE CAN BE PRETTY ANNOYING, BUT WHAT CAN I DO? SHE'S MY SISTER.
IF YOU DID, I WOULD JUST SHOW HIM ONE OF THESE BABIES.
CHEATER.
DANIEL, FIRST OFF, THIS STEAK IS FANTASTIC. BUT THE ALIEN YOU'RE GOING AFTER, NUMBER 7... NOT SO MUCH.
HE'S A REALLY, REALLY BAD GUY, AND THE LIST DOESN'T HAVE ANY INFORMATION ON HIS ABILITIES. YOU DON'T EVEN KNOW HIS SPECIES.
I'LL BE CAREFUL, DAD.
DON'T JUST BE CAREFUL, BE PARANOID. AND BE EXPECTING ME LATER. YOU'RE OVERDUE FOR ONE OF OUR TRAINING SESSIONS.
UM...OKAY, I'LL LOOK FORWARD TO IT. I GUESS.

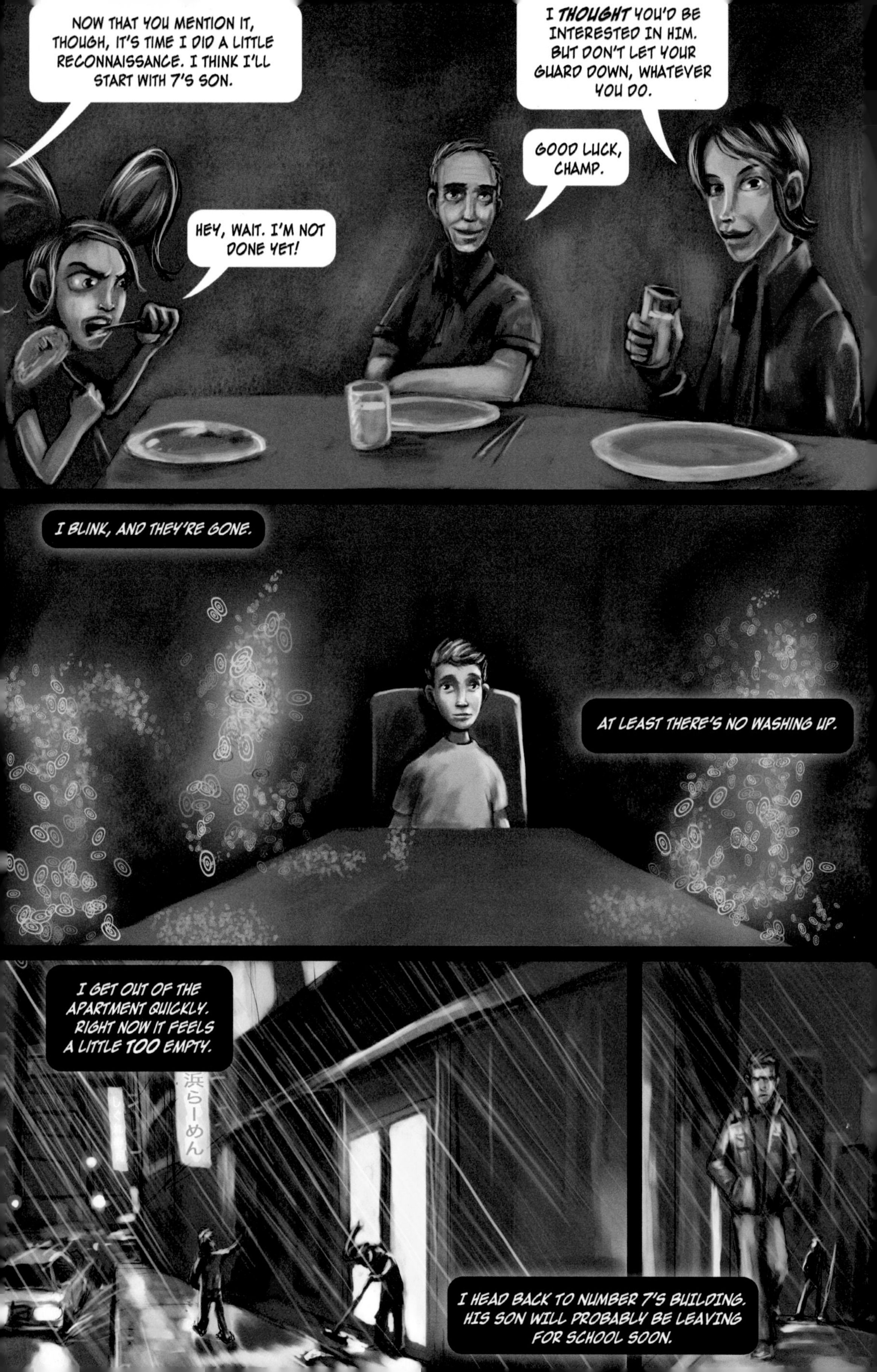
NOW THAT YOU MENTION IT, THOUGH, IT'S TIME I DID A LITTLE RECONNAISSANCE. I THINK I'LL START WITH 7'S SON.
I *THOUGHT* YOU'D BE INTERESTED IN HIM. BUT DON'T LET YOUR GUARD DOWN, WHATEVER YOU DO.
GOOD LUCK, CHAMP.
HEY, WAIT. I'M NOT DONE YET!
I BLINK, AND THEY'RE GONE.
AT LEAST THERE'S NO WASHING UP.
I GET OUT OF THE APARTMENT QUICKLY. RIGHT NOW IT FEELS A LITTLE **TOO** EMPTY.
浜らーめん
I HEAD BACK TO NUMBER 7'S BUILDING. HIS SON WILL PROBABLY BE LEAVING FOR SCHOOL SOON.

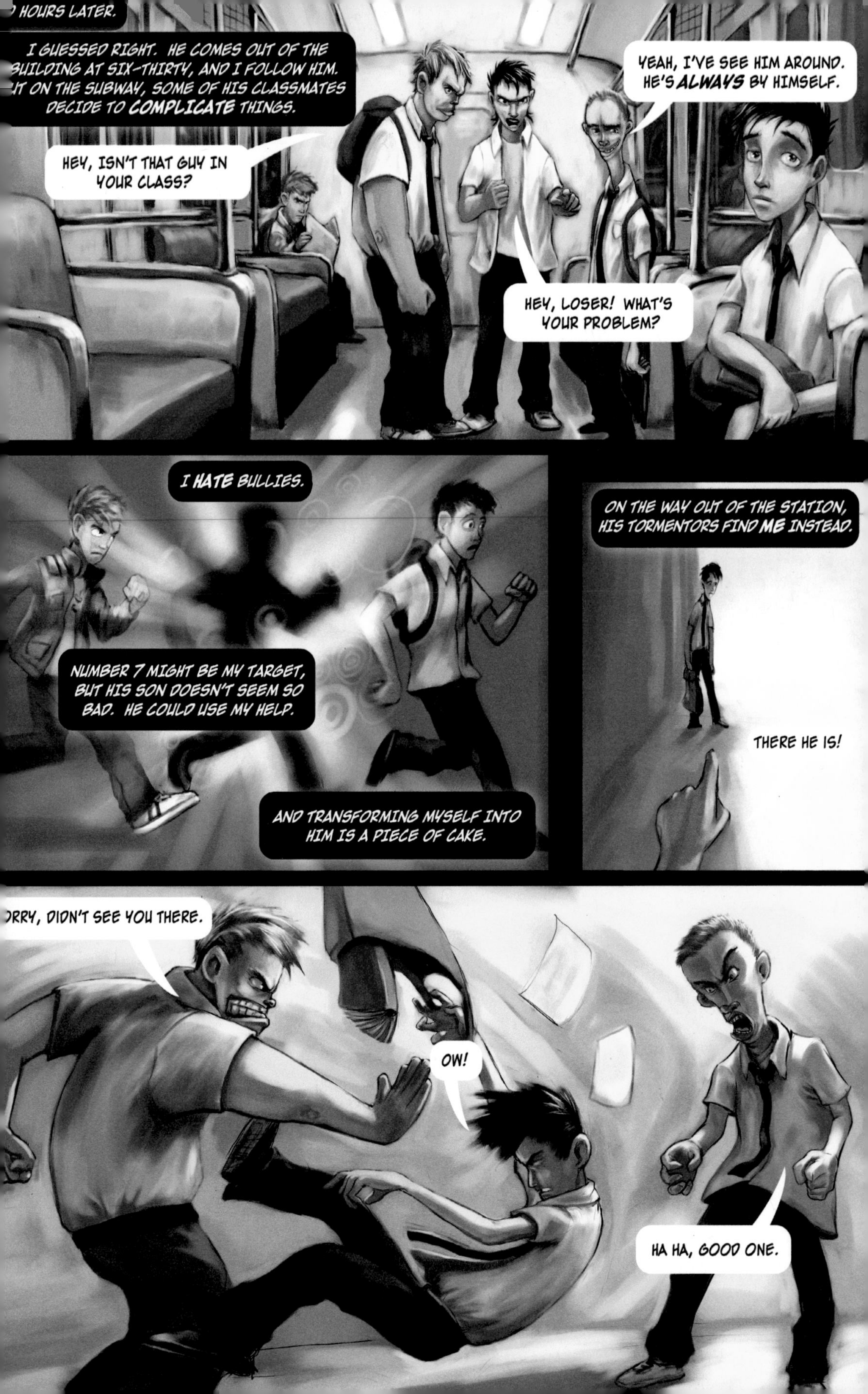

HOURS LATER.
I GUESSED RIGHT. HE COMES OUT OF THE BUILDING AT SIX-THIRTY, AND I FOLLOW HIM. UT ON THE SUBWAY, SOME OF HIS CLASSMATES DECIDE TO COMPLICATE THINGS.
HEY, ISN'T THAT GUY IN YOUR CLASS?
YEAH, I'VE SEE HIM AROUND. HE'S ALWAYS BY HIMSELF.
HEY, LOSER! WHAT'S YOUR PROBLEM?
I HATE BULLIES.
NUMBER 7 MIGHT BE MY TARGET, BUT HIS SON DOESN'T SEEM SO BAD. HE COULD USE MY HELP.
AND TRANSFORMING MYSELF INTO HIM IS A PIECE OF CAKE.
ON THE WAY OUT OF THE STATION, HIS TORMENTORS FIND ME INSTEAD.
THERE HE IS!
RRY, DIDN'T SEE YOU THERE.
OW!
HA HA, GOOD ONE.

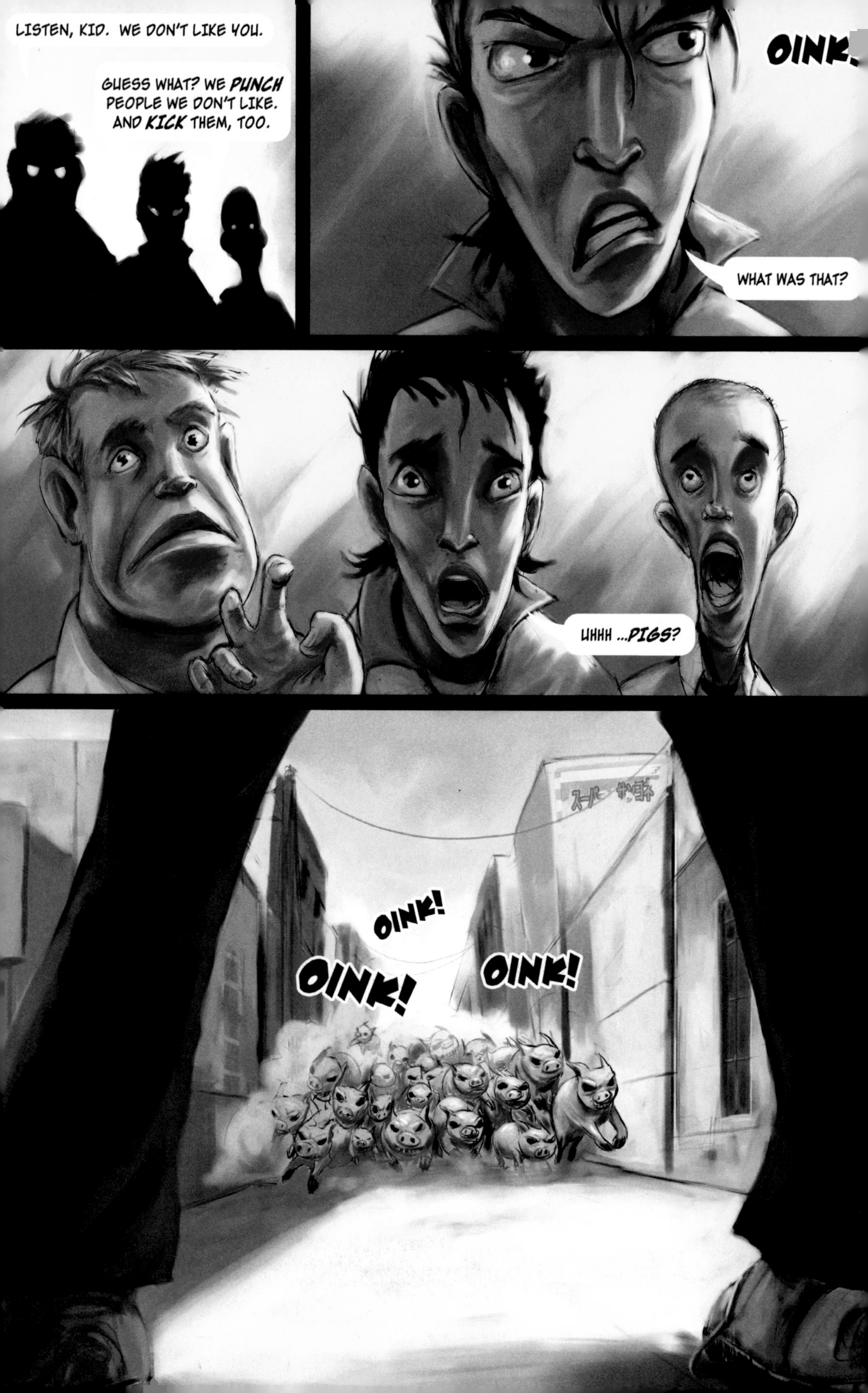
LISTEN, KID. WE DON'T LIKE YOU.
GUESS WHAT? WE PUNCH PEOPLE WE DON'T LIKE. AND KICK THEM, TOO.
OINK!
WHAT WAS THAT?
UHHH ...PIGS?
スーパー サンヨネ
OINK!
OINK!
OINK!

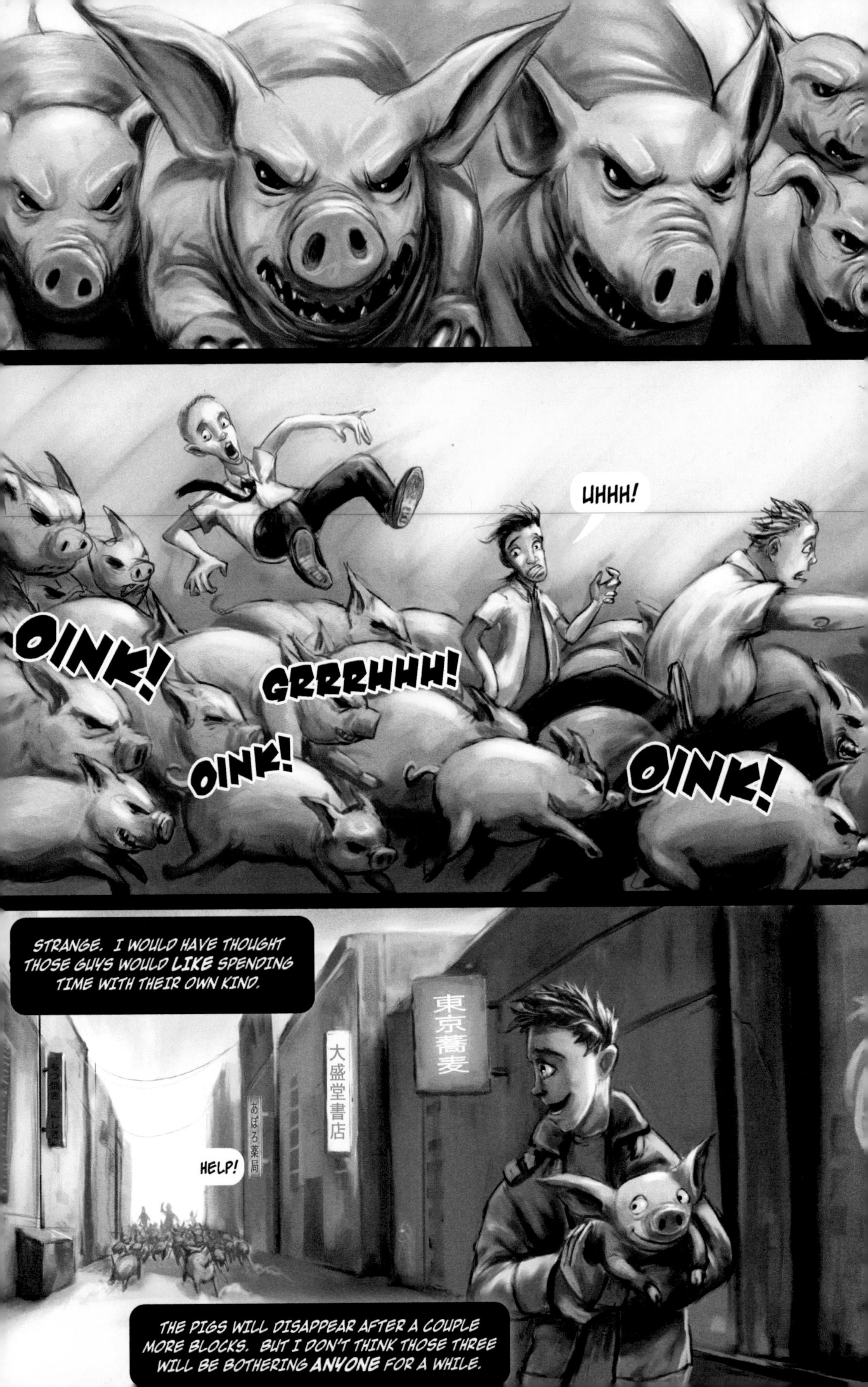
UHHH!
OINK!
GRRRHHH!
OINK!
OINK!
STRANGE. I WOULD HAVE THOUGHT THOSE GUYS WOULD **LIKE** SPENDING TIME WITH THEIR OWN KIND.
東京蕎麦
大盛堂書店
あぼろ薬局
HELP!
THE PIGS WILL DISAPPEAR AFTER A COUPLE MORE BLOCKS. BUT I DON'T THINK THOSE THREE WILL BE BOTHERING **ANYONE** FOR A WHILE.

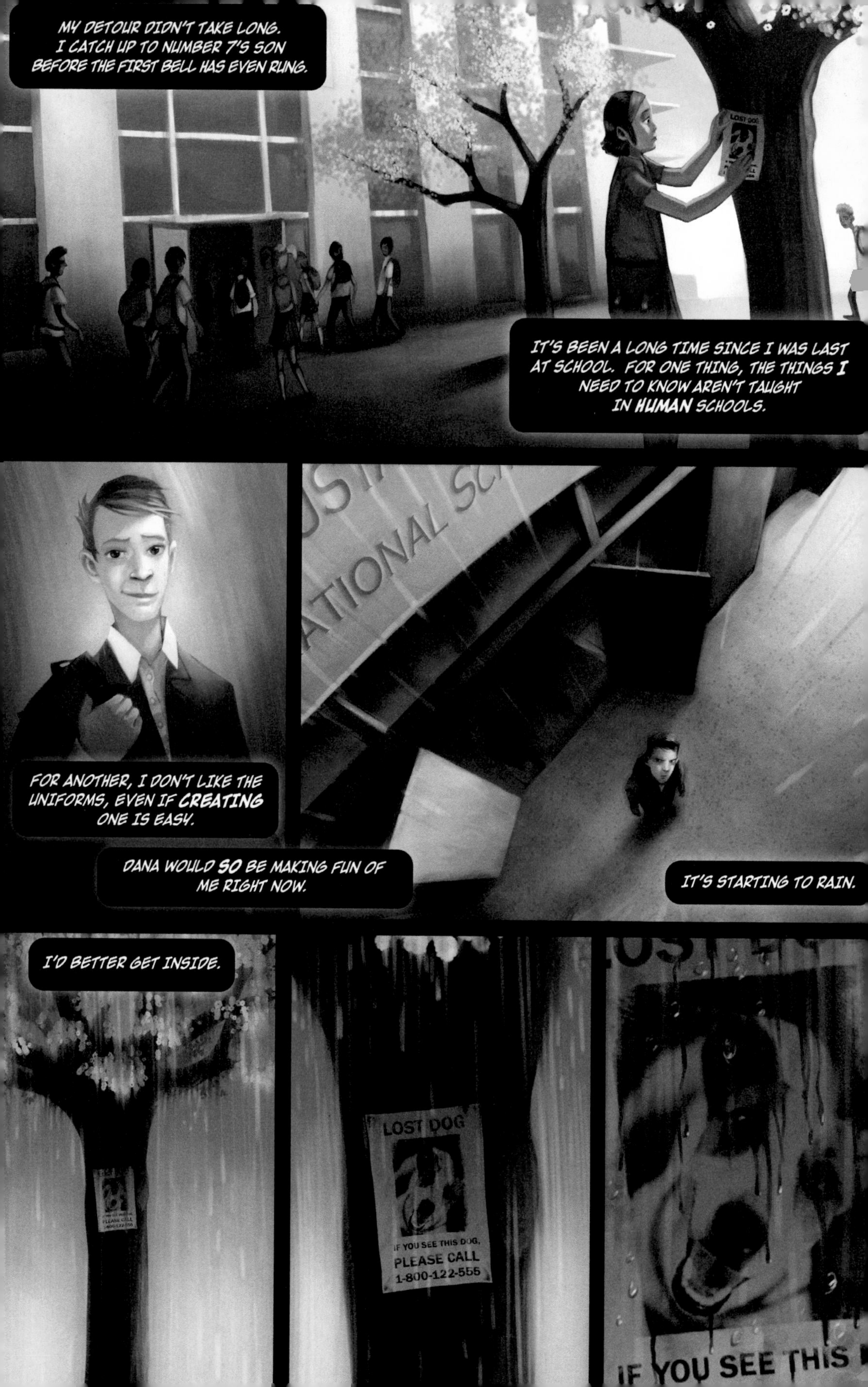
MY DETOUR DIDN'T TAKE LONG. I CATCH UP TO NUMBER 7'S SON BEFORE THE FIRST BELL HAS EVEN RUNG.
LOST DOG
IT'S BEEN A LONG TIME SINCE I WAS LAST AT SCHOOL. FOR ONE THING, THE THINGS I NEED TO KNOW AREN'T TAUGHT IN HUMAN SCHOOLS.
FOR ANOTHER, I DON'T LIKE THE UNIFORMS, EVEN IF CREATING ONE IS EASY.
ATIONAL SC
DANA WOULD SO BE MAKING FUN OF ME RIGHT NOW.
IT'S STARTING TO RAIN.
I'D BETTER GET INSIDE.
LOST DOG
IF YOU SEE THIS DOG, PLEASE CALL 1-800-122-555
IF YOU SEE THIS

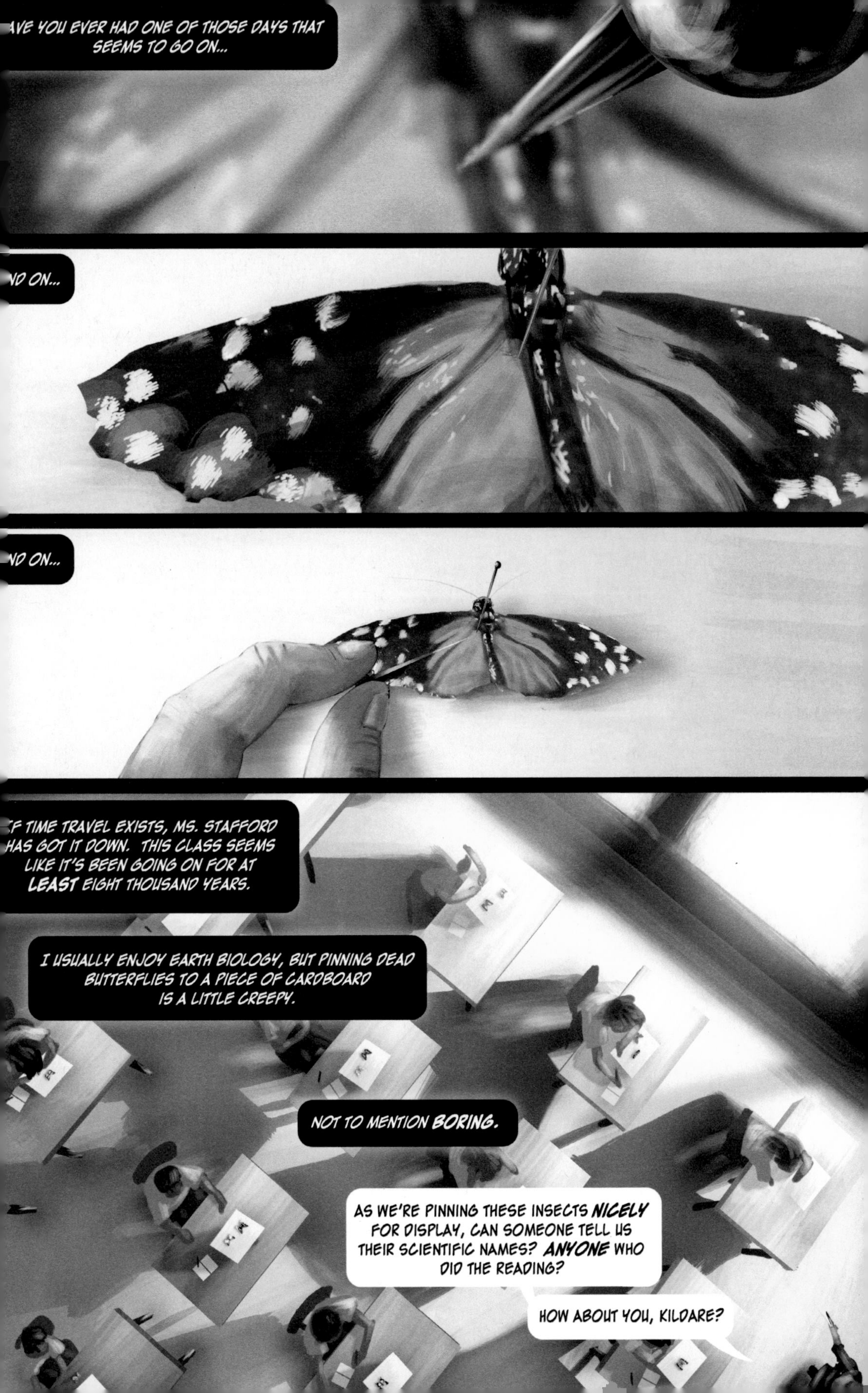

AVE YOU EVER HAD ONE OF THOSE DAYS THAT SEEMS TO GO ON...
ND ON...
ND ON...
F TIME TRAVEL EXISTS, MS. STAFFORD HAS GOT IT DOWN. THIS CLASS SEEMS LIKE IT'S BEEN GOING ON FOR AT LEAST EIGHT THOUSAND YEARS.
I USUALLY ENJOY EARTH BIOLOGY, BUT PINNING DEAD BUTTERFLIES TO A PIECE OF CARDBOARD IS A LITTLE CREEPY.
NOT TO MENTION BORING.
AS WE'RE PINNING THESE INSECTS NICELY FOR DISPLAY, CAN SOMEONE TELL US THEIR SCIENTIFIC NAMES? ANYONE WHO DID THE READING?
HOW ABOUT YOU, KILDARE?

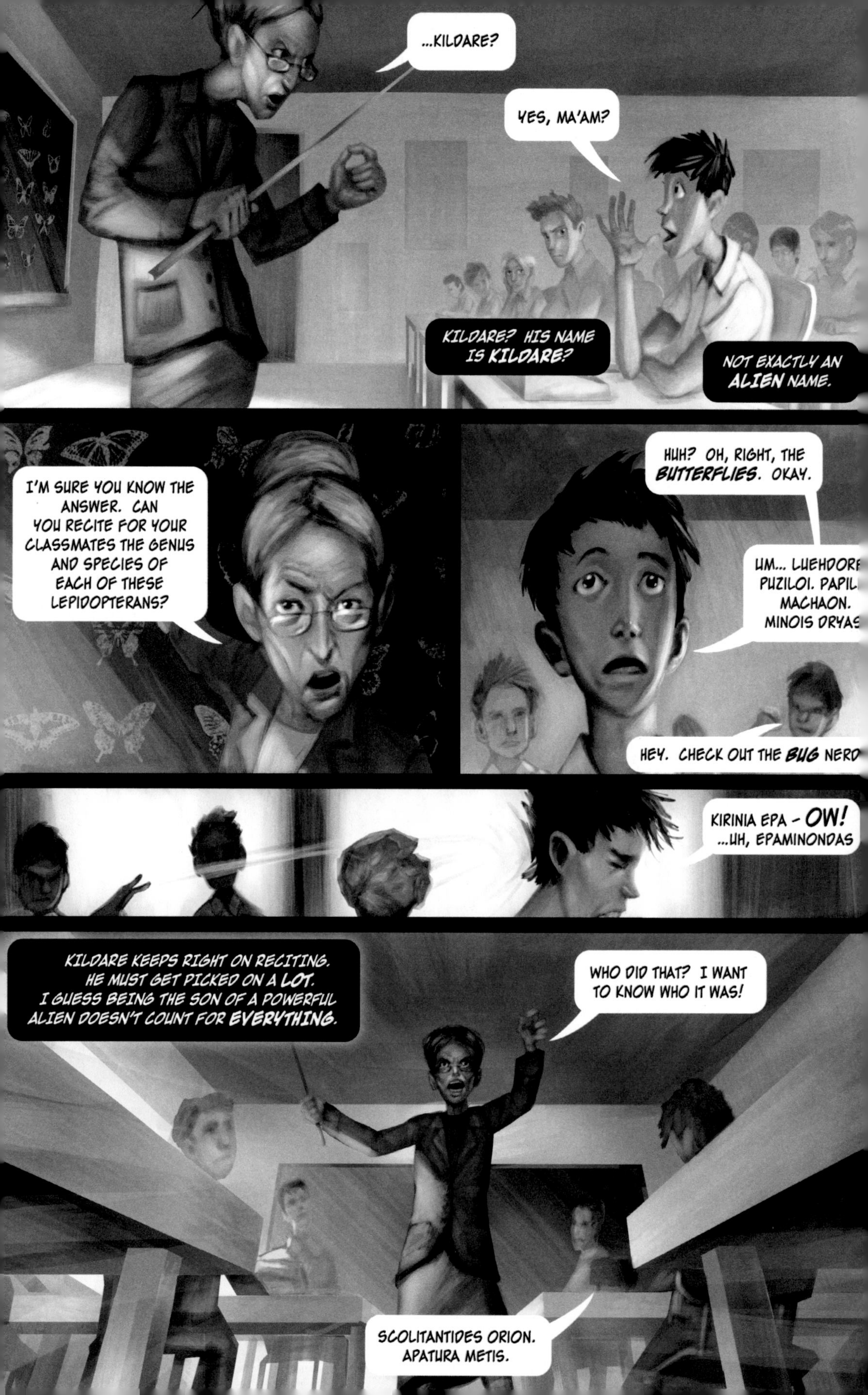
...KILDARE?
YES, MA'AM?
KILDARE? HIS NAME IS KILDARE?
NOT EXACTLY AN ALIEN NAME.
I'M SURE YOU KNOW THE ANSWER. CAN YOU RECITE FOR YOUR CLASSMATES THE GENUS AND SPECIES OF EACH OF THESE LEPIDOPTERANS?
HUH? OH, RIGHT, THE BUTTERFLIES. OKAY.
UM... LUEHDORF PUZILOI. PAPIL MACHAON. MINOIS DRYAS
HEY. CHECK OUT THE BUG NERD
KIRINIA EPA - OW! ...UH, EPAMINONDAS
KILDARE KEEPS RIGHT ON RECITING. HE MUST GET PICKED ON A LOT. I GUESS BEING THE SON OF A POWERFUL ALIEN DOESN'T COUNT FOR EVERYTHING.
WHO DID THAT? I WANT TO KNOW WHO IT WAS!
SCOLITANTIDES ORION. APATURA METIS.

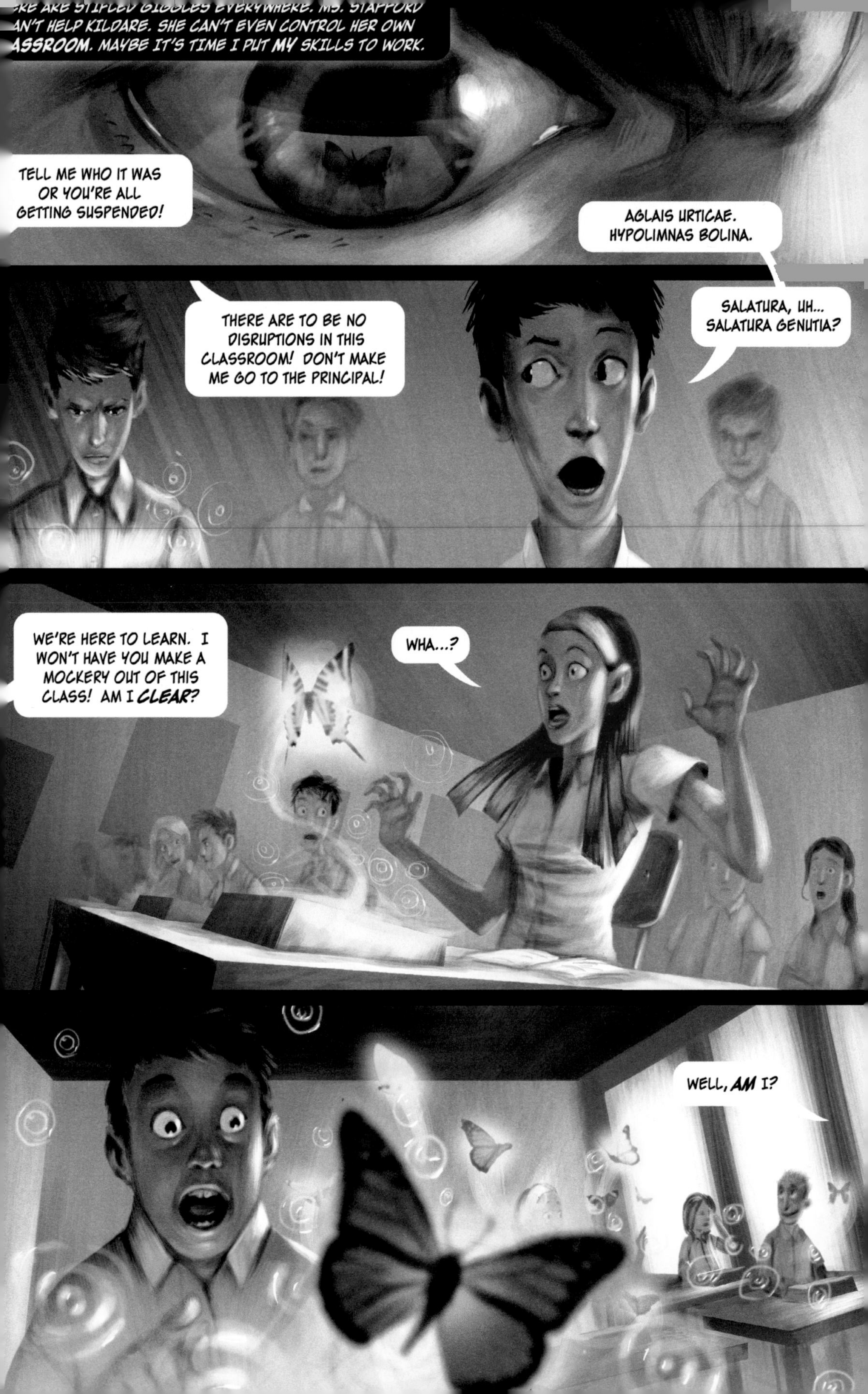

ERE ARE STIFLED GIGGLES EVERYWHERE. MS. STAFFORD AN'T HELP KILDARE. SHE CAN'T EVEN CONTROL HER OWN ASSROOM. MAYBE IT'S TIME I PUT MY SKILLS TO WORK.
TELL ME WHO IT WAS OR YOU'RE ALL GETTING SUSPENDED!
AGLAIS URTICAE. HYPOLIMNAS BOLINA.
THERE ARE TO BE NO DISRUPTIONS IN THIS CLASSROOM! DON'T MAKE ME GO TO THE PRINCIPAL!
SALATURA, UH... SALATURA GENUTIA?
WE'RE HERE TO LEARN. I WON'T HAVE YOU MAKE A MOCKERY OUT OF THIS CLASS! AM I CLEAR?
WHA...?
WELL, AM I?

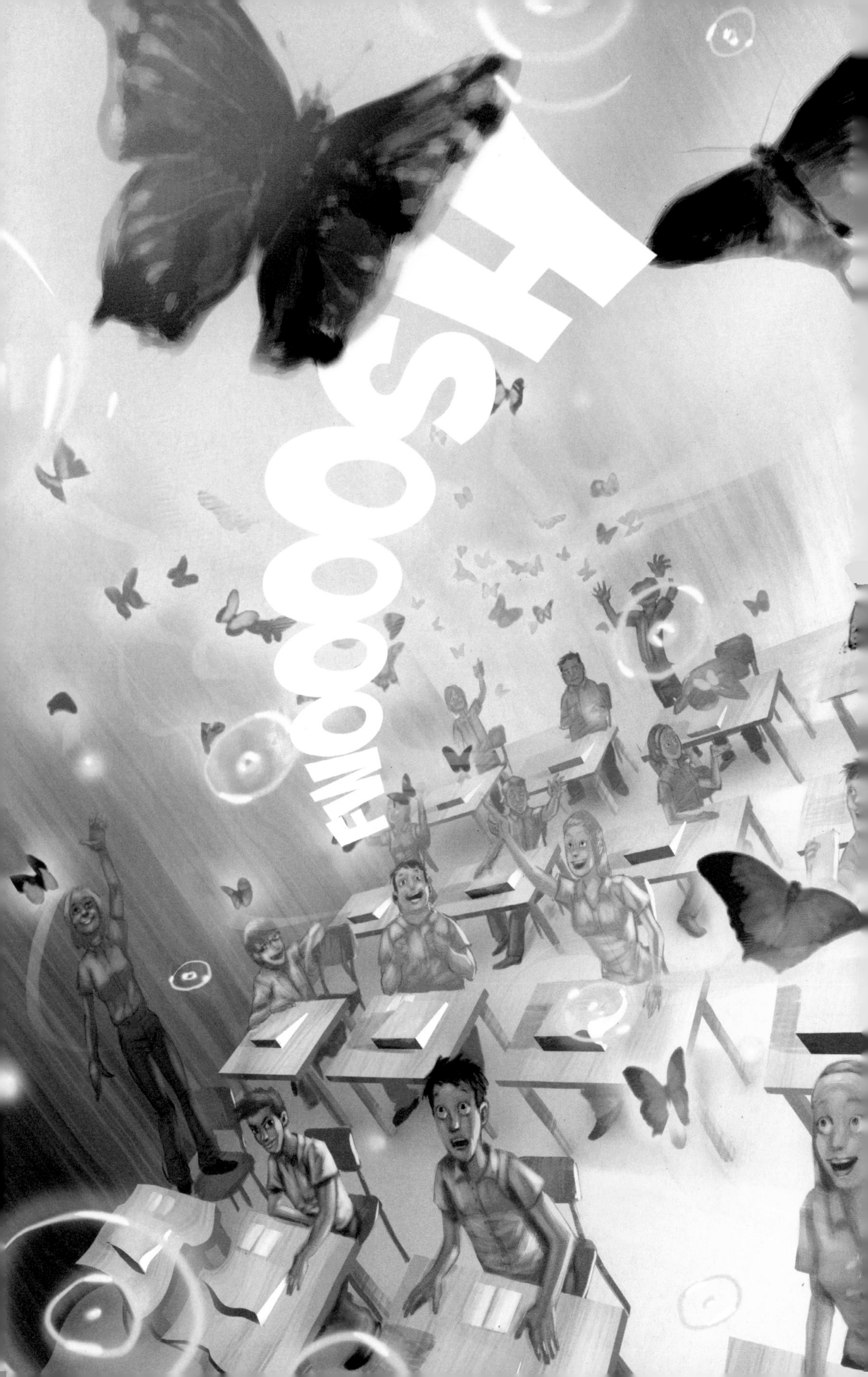
FWOOOOSH

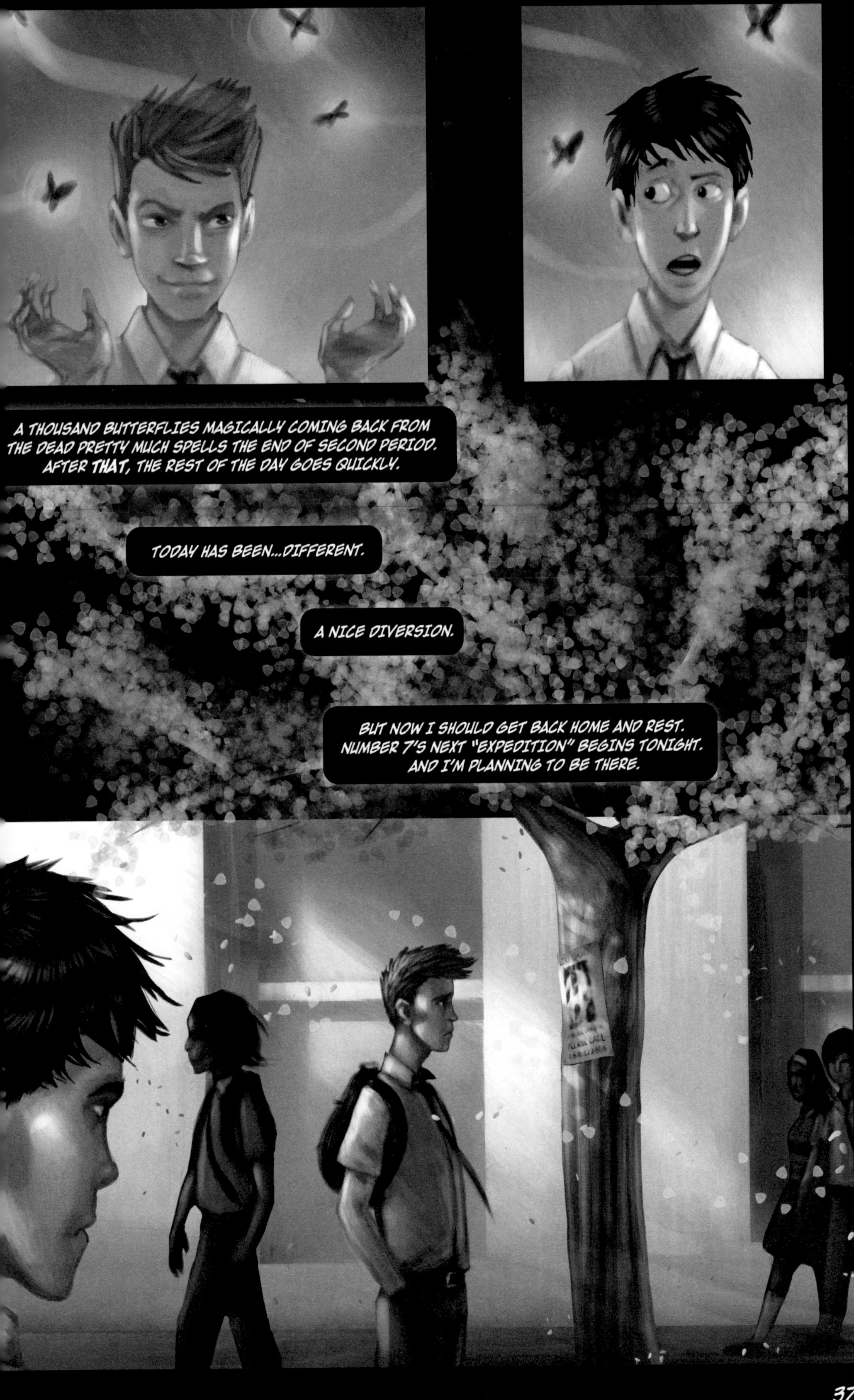
A THOUSAND BUTTERFLIES MAGICALLY COMING BACK FROM THE DEAD PRETTY MUCH SPELLS THE END OF SECOND PERIOD. AFTER THAT, THE REST OF THE DAY GOES QUICKLY.
TODAY HAS BEEN...DIFFERENT.
A NICE DIVERSION.
BUT NOW I SHOULD GET BACK HOME AND REST. NUMBER 7'S NEXT "EXPEDITION" BEGINS TONIGHT. AND I'M PLANNING TO BE THERE.

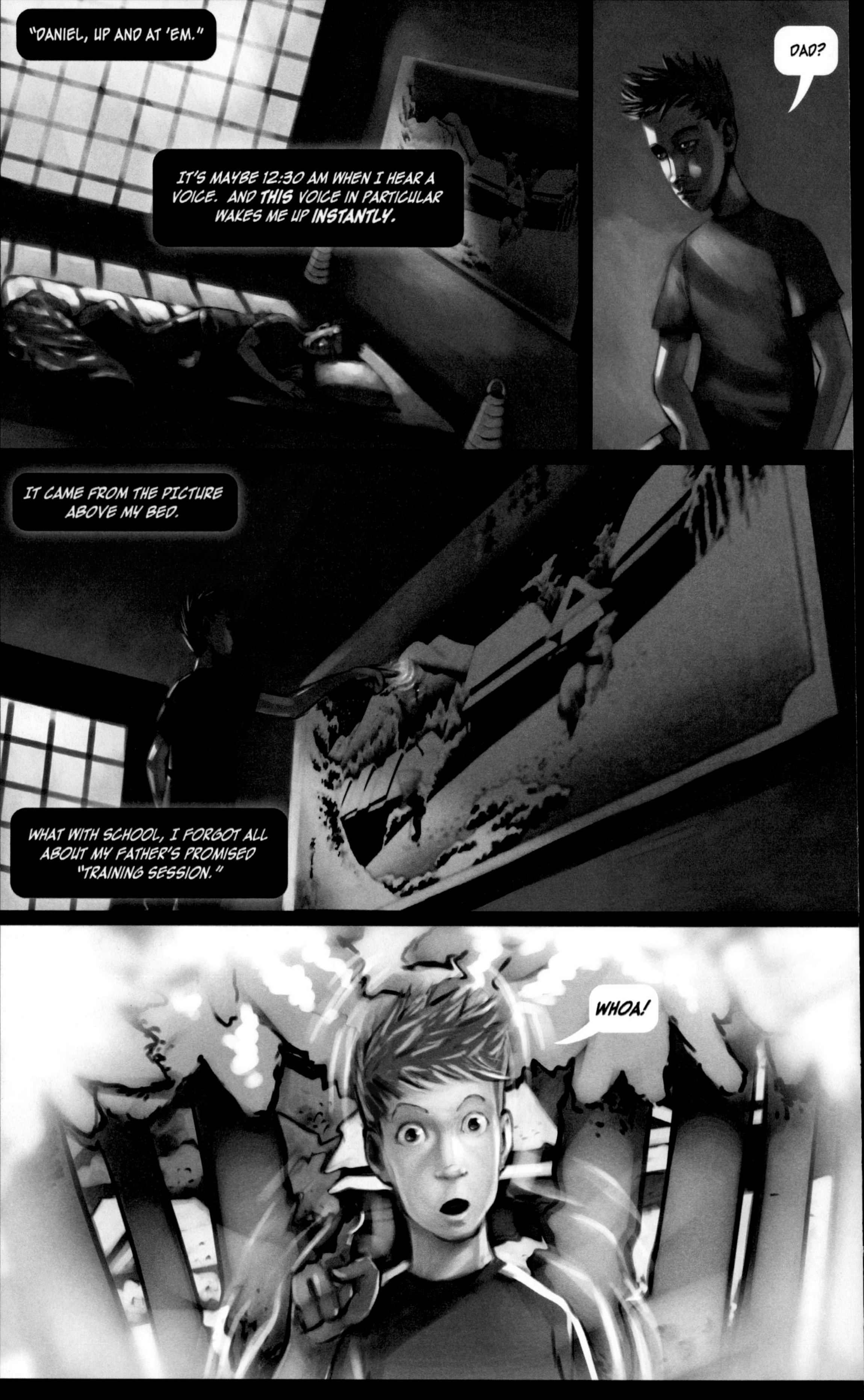
"DANIEL, UP AND AT 'EM."
IT'S MAYBE 12:30 AM WHEN I HEAR A VOICE. AND THIS VOICE IN PARTICULAR WAKES ME UP INSTANTLY.
DAD?
IT CAME FROM THE PICTURE ABOVE MY BED.
WHAT WITH SCHOOL, I FORGOT ALL ABOUT MY FATHER'S PROMISED "TRAINING SESSION."
WHOA!

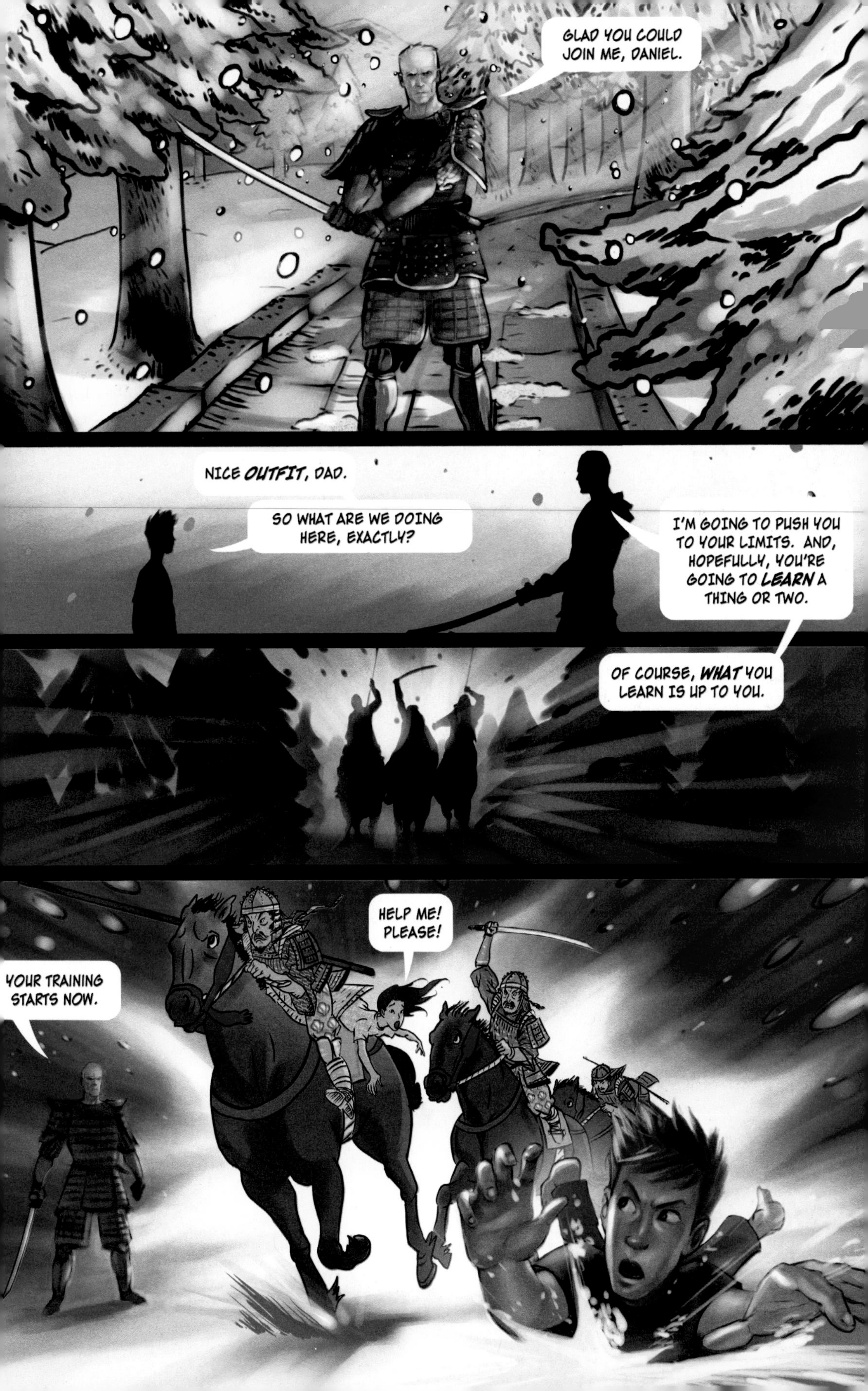
GLAD YOU COULD JOIN ME, DANIEL.
NICE OUTFIT, DAD.
SO WHAT ARE WE DOING HERE, EXACTLY?
I'M GOING TO PUSH YOU TO YOUR LIMITS. AND, HOPEFULLY, YOU'RE GOING TO LEARN A THING OR TWO.
OF COURSE, WHAT YOU LEARN IS UP TO YOU.
HELP ME! PLEASE!
YOUR TRAINING STARTS NOW.

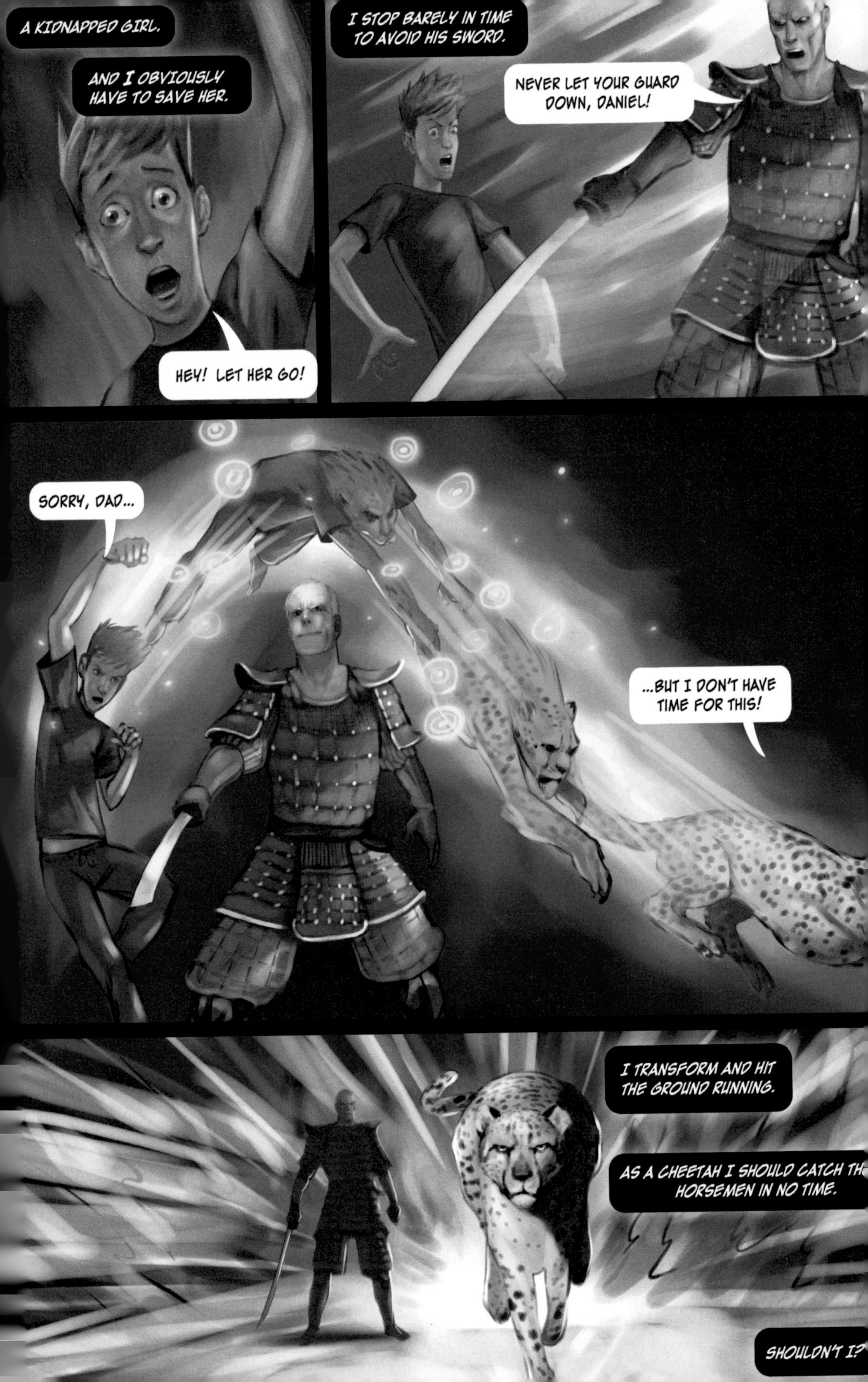
A KIDNAPPED GIRL.
AND I OBVIOUSLY HAVE TO SAVE HER.
HEY! LET HER GO!
I STOP BARELY IN TIME TO AVOID HIS SWORD.
NEVER LET YOUR GUARD DOWN, DANIEL!
SORRY, DAD...
...BUT I DON'T HAVE TIME FOR THIS!
I TRANSFORM AND HIT THE GROUND RUNNING.
AS A CHEETAH I SHOULD CATCH TH
HORSEMEN IN NO TIME.
SHOULDN'T I?

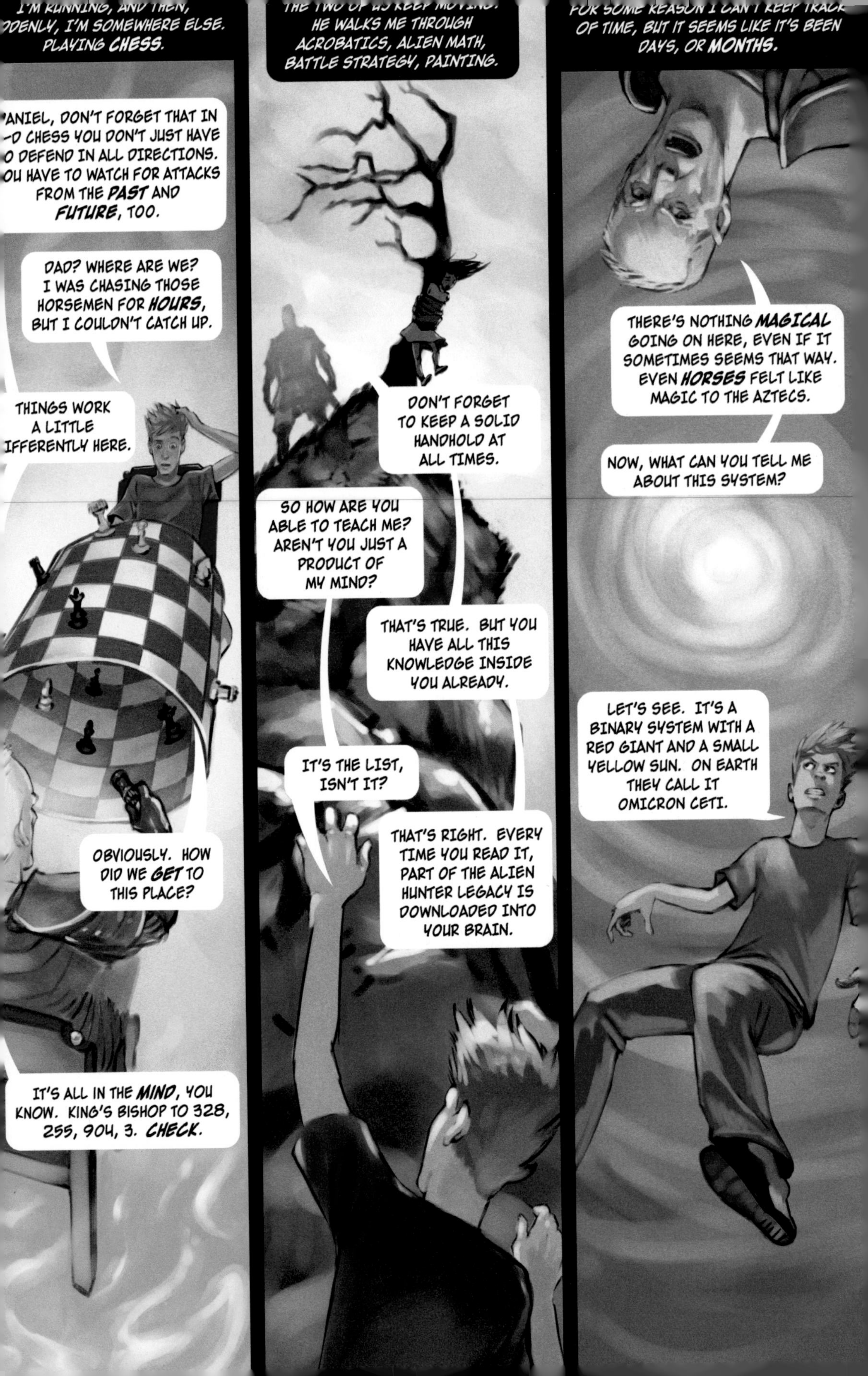
I'M RUNNING, AND THEN,
DDENLY, I'M SOMEWHERE ELSE. PLAYING CHESS.
ANIEL, DON'T FORGET THAT IN -D CHESS YOU DON'T JUST HAVE O DEFEND IN ALL DIRECTIONS. OU HAVE TO WATCH FOR ATTACKS FROM THE PAST AND FUTURE, TOO.
DAD? WHERE ARE WE? I WAS CHASING THOSE HORSEMEN FOR HOURS, BUT I COULDN'T CATCH UP.
THINGS WORK A LITTLE IFFERENTLY HERE.
OBVIOUSLY. HOW DID WE GET TO THIS PLACE?
IT'S ALL IN THE MIND, YOU KNOW. KING'S BISHOP TO 328, 255, 904, 3. CHECK.
HE WALKS ME THROUGH ACROBATICS, ALIEN MATH, BATTLE STRATEGY, PAINTING.
DON'T FORGET TO KEEP A SOLID HANDHOLD AT ALL TIMES.
SO HOW ARE YOU ABLE TO TEACH ME? AREN'T YOU JUST A PRODUCT OF MY MIND?
THAT'S TRUE. BUT YOU HAVE ALL THIS KNOWLEDGE INSIDE YOU ALREADY.
IT'S THE LIST, ISN'T IT?
THAT'S RIGHT. EVERY TIME YOU READ IT, PART OF THE ALIEN HUNTER LEGACY IS DOWNLOADED INTO YOUR BRAIN.
OF TIME, BUT IT SEEMS LIKE IT'S BEEN DAYS, OR MONTHS.
THERE'S NOTHING MAGICAL GOING ON HERE, EVEN IF IT SOMETIMES SEEMS THAT WAY. EVEN HORSES FELT LIKE MAGIC TO THE AZTECS.
NOW, WHAT CAN YOU TELL ME ABOUT THIS SYSTEM?
LET'S SEE. IT'S A BINARY SYSTEM WITH A RED GIANT AND A SMALL YELLOW SUN. ON EARTH THEY CALL IT OMICRON CETI.

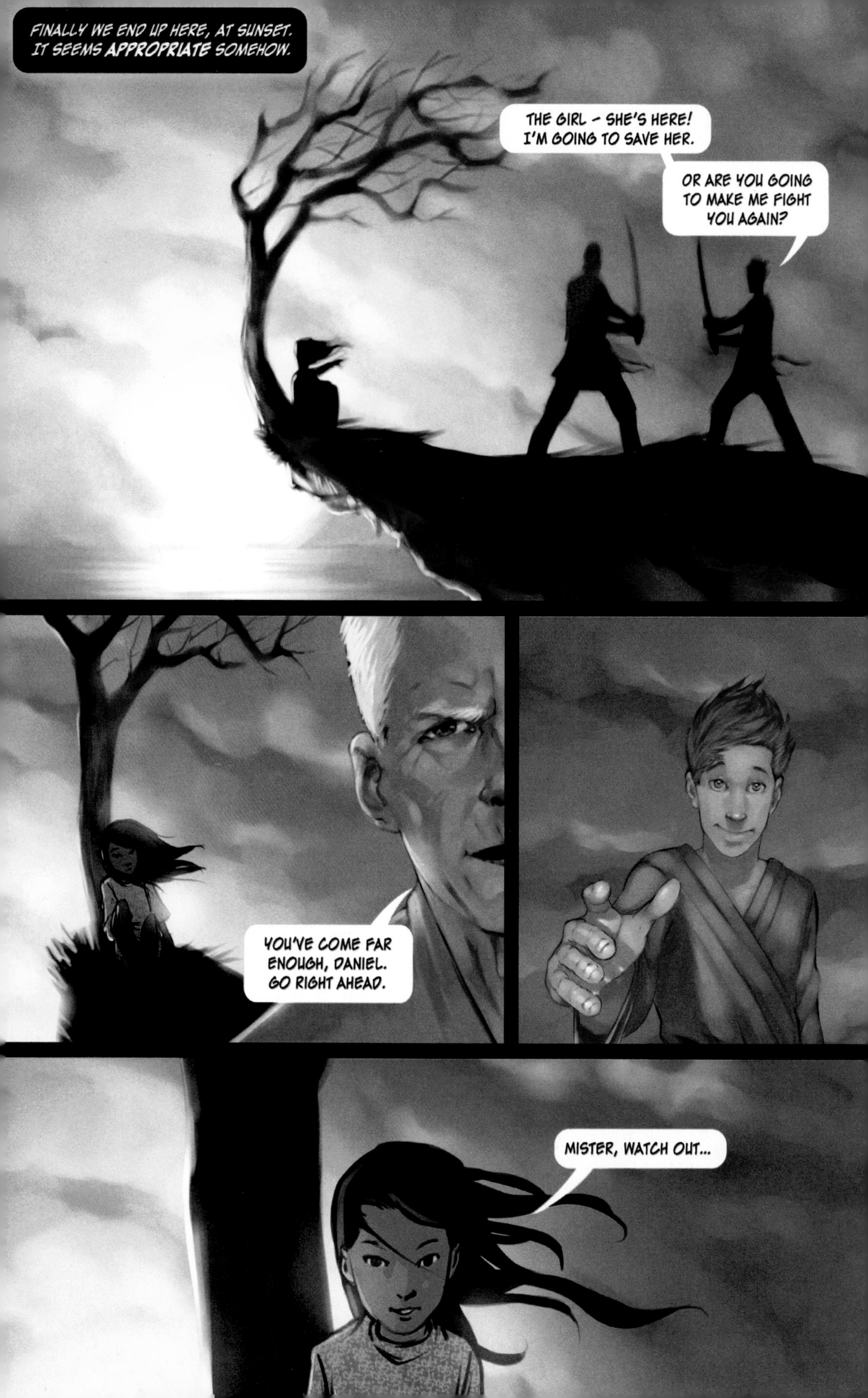
FINALLY WE END UP HERE, AT SUNSET. IT SEEMS APPROPRIATE SOMEHOW.
THE GIRL - SHE'S HERE! I'M GOING TO SAVE HER.
OR ARE YOU GOING TO MAKE ME FIGHT YOU AGAIN?
YOU'VE COME FAR ENOUGH, DANIEL. GO RIGHT AHEAD.
MISTER, WATCH OUT...

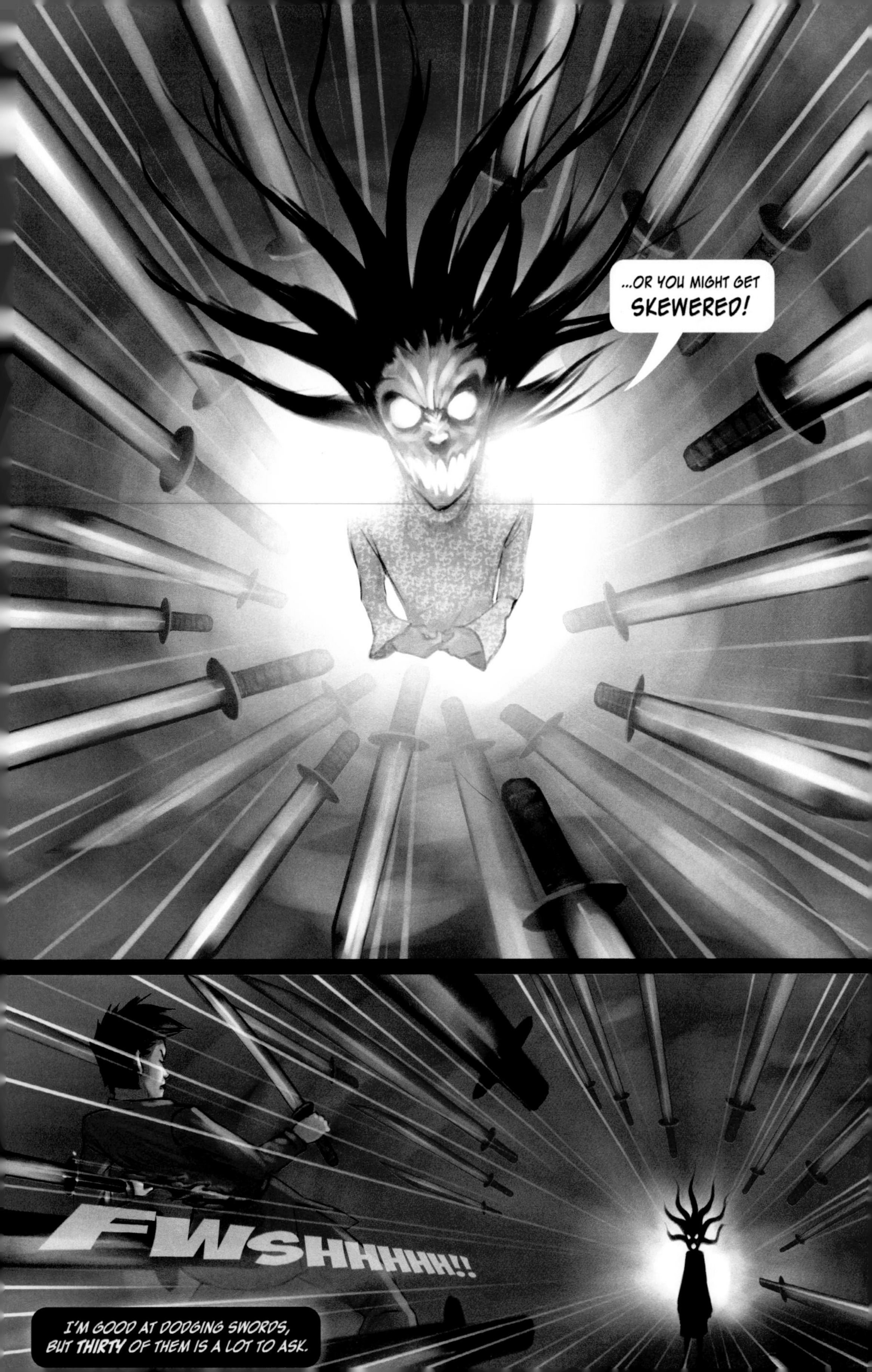

...OR YOU MIGHT GET SKEWERED!
FWSHHHHH!!
I'M GOOD AT DODGING SWORDS, BUT THIRTY OF THEM IS A LOT TO ASK.

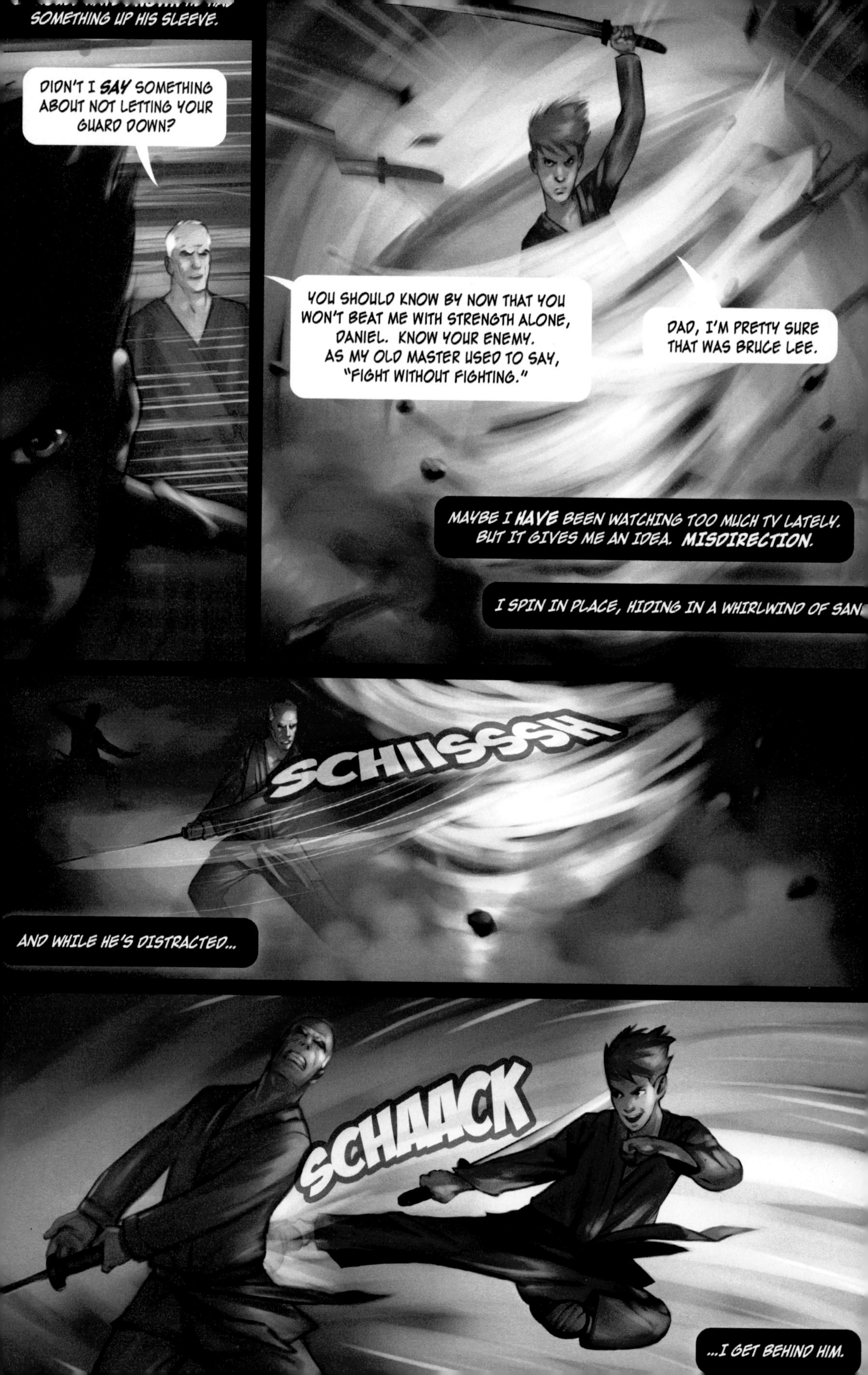
SOMETHING UP HIS SLEEVE.
DIDN'T I SAY SOMETHING ABOUT NOT LETTING YOUR GUARD DOWN?
YOU SHOULD KNOW BY NOW THAT YOU WON'T BEAT ME WITH STRENGTH ALONE, DANIEL. KNOW YOUR ENEMY. AS MY OLD MASTER USED TO SAY, "FIGHT WITHOUT FIGHTING."
DAD, I'M PRETTY SURE THAT WAS BRUCE LEE.
MAYBE I HAVE BEEN WATCHING TOO MUCH TV LATELY. BUT IT GIVES ME AN IDEA. MISDIRECTION.
I SPIN IN PLACE, HIDING IN A WHIRLWIND OF SAN
SCHIISSSH
AND WHILE HE'S DISTRACTED...
SCHAACK
...I GET BEHIND HIM.

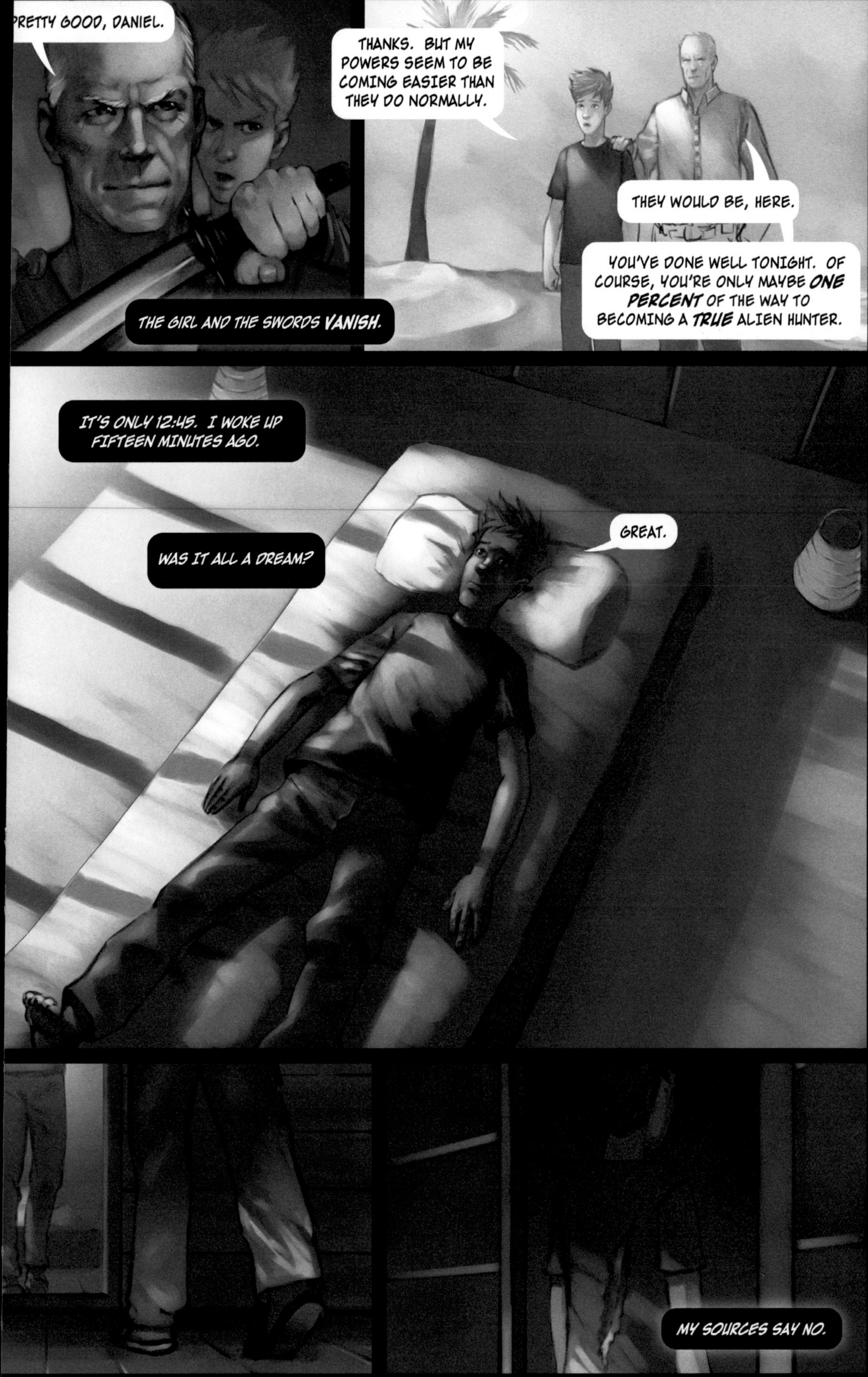
PRETTY GOOD, DANIEL.
THE GIRL AND THE SWORDS VANISH.
THANKS. BUT MY POWERS SEEM TO BE COMING EASIER THAN THEY DO NORMALLY.
THEY WOULD BE, HERE.
YOU'VE DONE WELL TONIGHT. OF COURSE, YOU'RE ONLY MAYBE ONE PERCENT OF THE WAY TO BECOMING A TRUE ALIEN HUNTER.
IT'S ONLY 12:45. I WOKE UP FIFTEEN MINUTES AGO.
WAS IT ALL A DREAM?
GREAT.
MY SOURCES SAY NO.

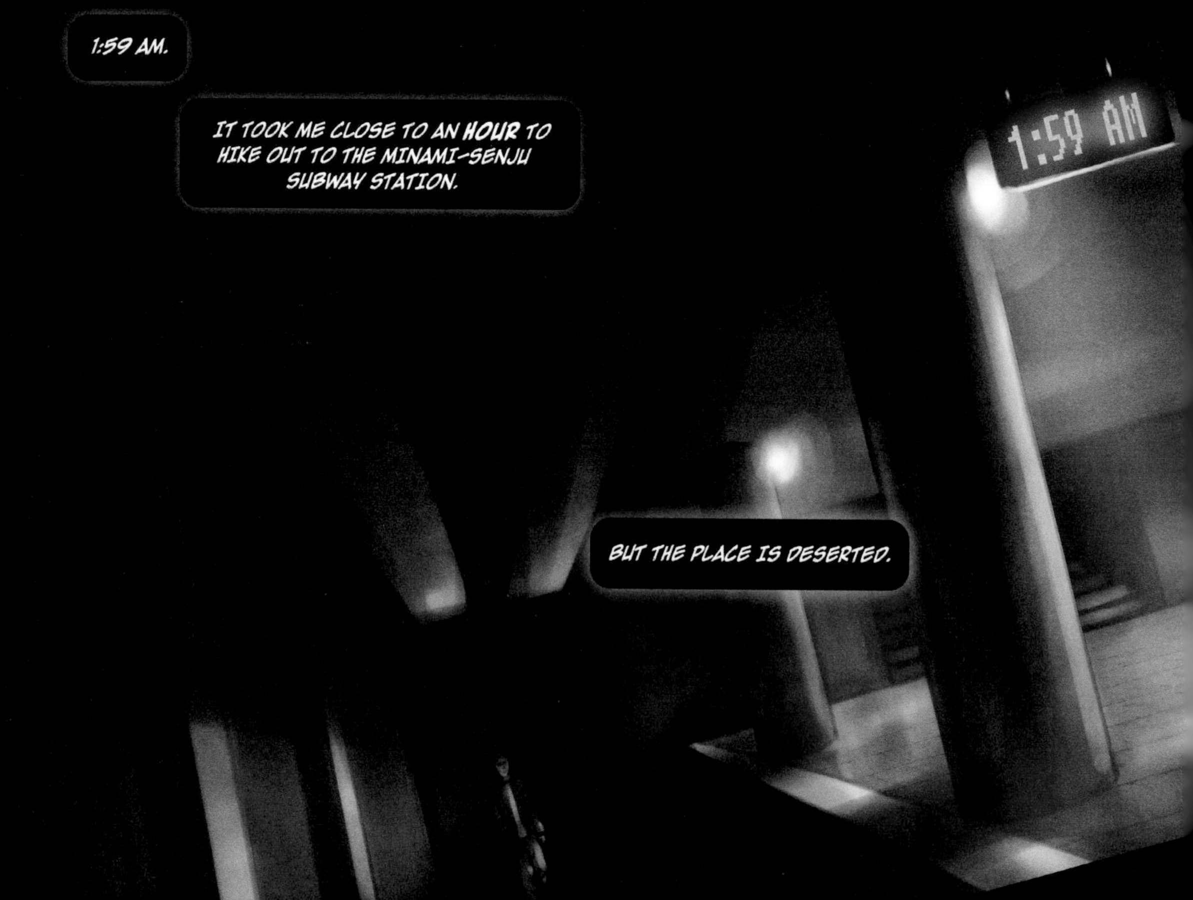
1:59 AM.
IT TOOK ME CLOSE TO AN HOUR TO HIKE OUT TO THE MINAMI-SENJU SUBWAY STATION.
1:59 AM
BUT THE PLACE IS DESERTED.

CHAPTER 3

THRILL OF THE CHASE

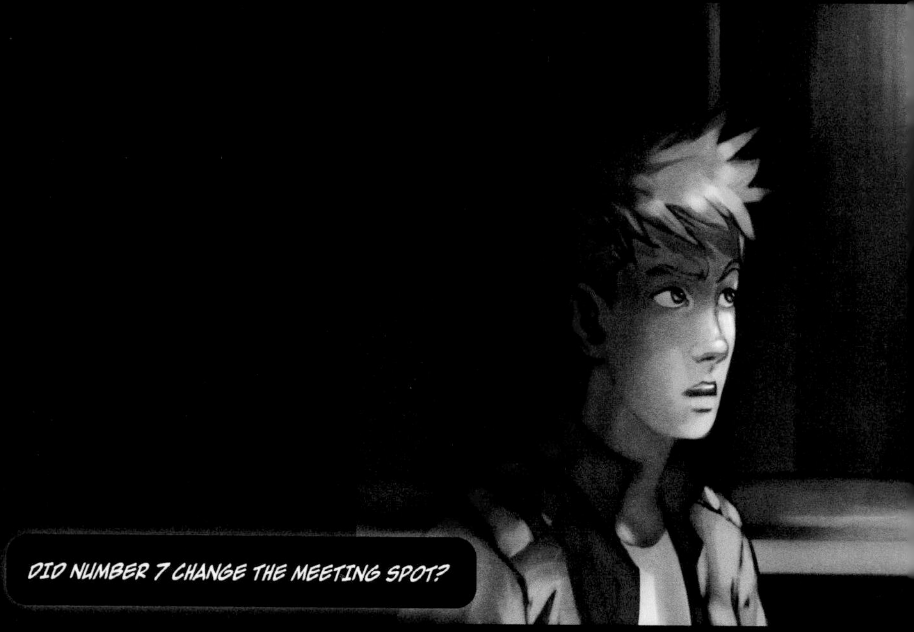
DID NUMBER 7 CHANGE THE MEETING SPOT?

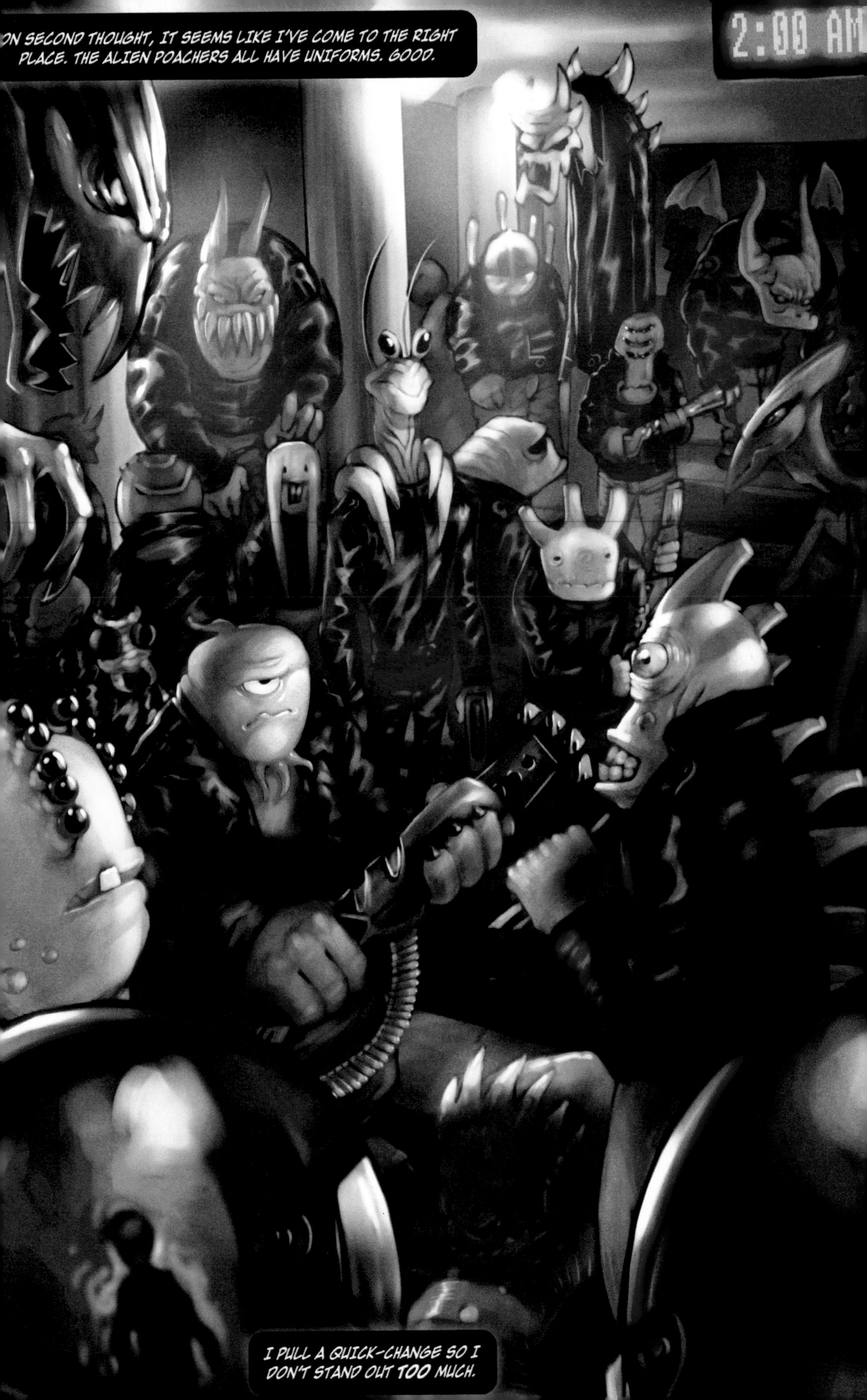
ON SECOND THOUGHT, IT SEEMS LIKE I'VE COME TO THE RIGHT PLACE. THE ALIEN POACHERS ALL HAVE UNIFORMS. GOOD.
2:00 AM
I PULL A QUICK-CHANGE SO I DON'T STAND OUT TOO MUCH.

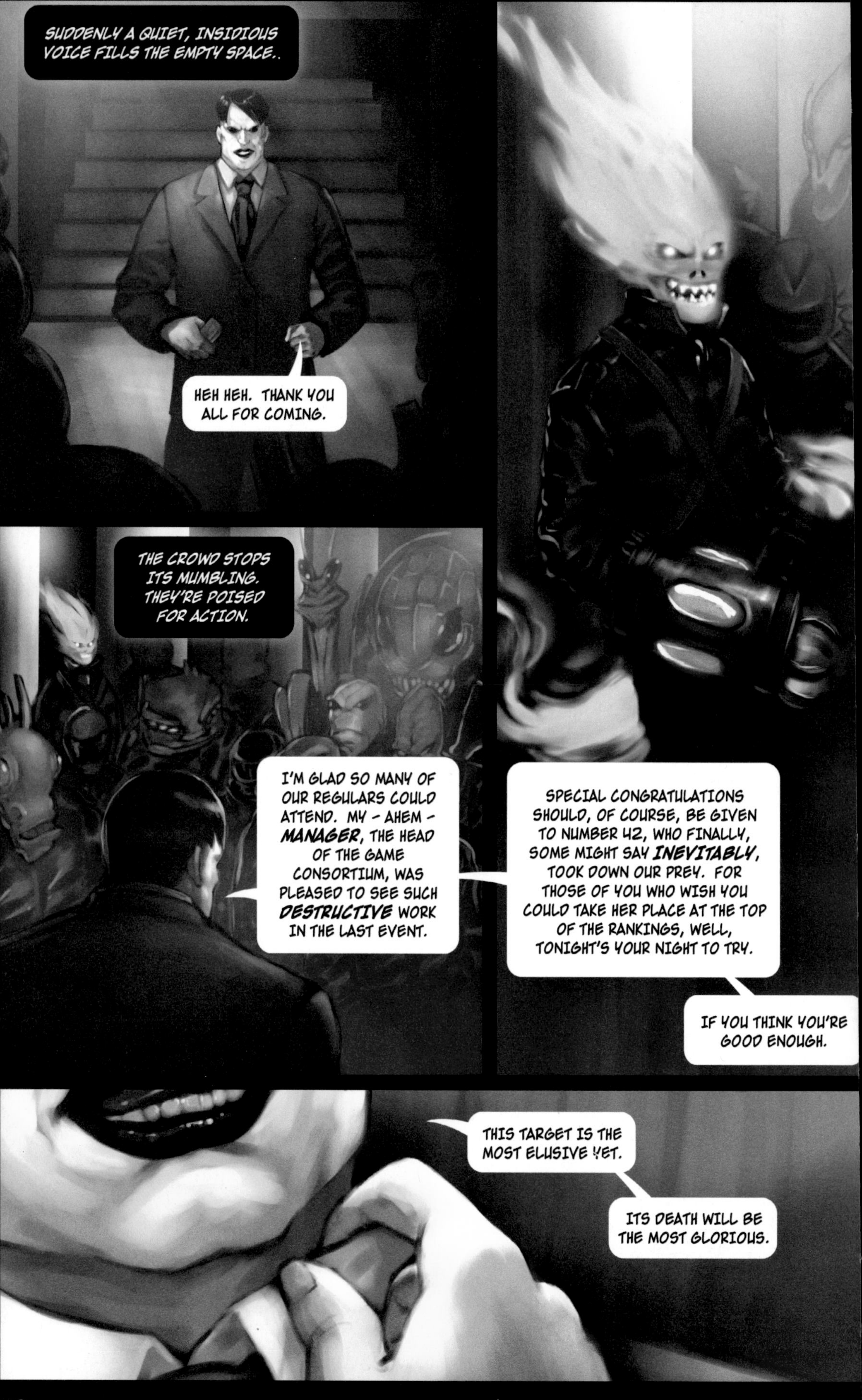
SUDDENLY A QUIET, INSIDIOUS VOICE FILLS THE EMPTY SPACE..
HEH HEH. THANK YOU ALL FOR COMING.
THE CROWD STOPS ITS MUMBLING. THEY'RE POISED FOR ACTION.
I'M GLAD SO MANY OF OUR REGULARS COULD ATTEND. MY - AHEM - MANAGER, THE HEAD OF THE GAME CONSORTIUM, WAS PLEASED TO SEE SUCH DESTRUCTIVE WORK IN THE LAST EVENT.
SPECIAL CONGRATULATIONS SHOULD, OF COURSE, BE GIVEN TO NUMBER 42, WHO FINALLY, SOME MIGHT SAY INEVITABLY, TOOK DOWN OUR PREY. FOR THOSE OF YOU WHO WISH YOU COULD TAKE HER PLACE AT THE TOP OF THE RANKINGS, WELL, TONIGHT'S YOUR NIGHT TO TRY.
IF YOU THINK YOU'RE GOOD ENOUGH.
THIS TARGET IS THE MOST ELUSIVE YET.
ITS DEATH WILL BE THE MOST GLORIOUS.

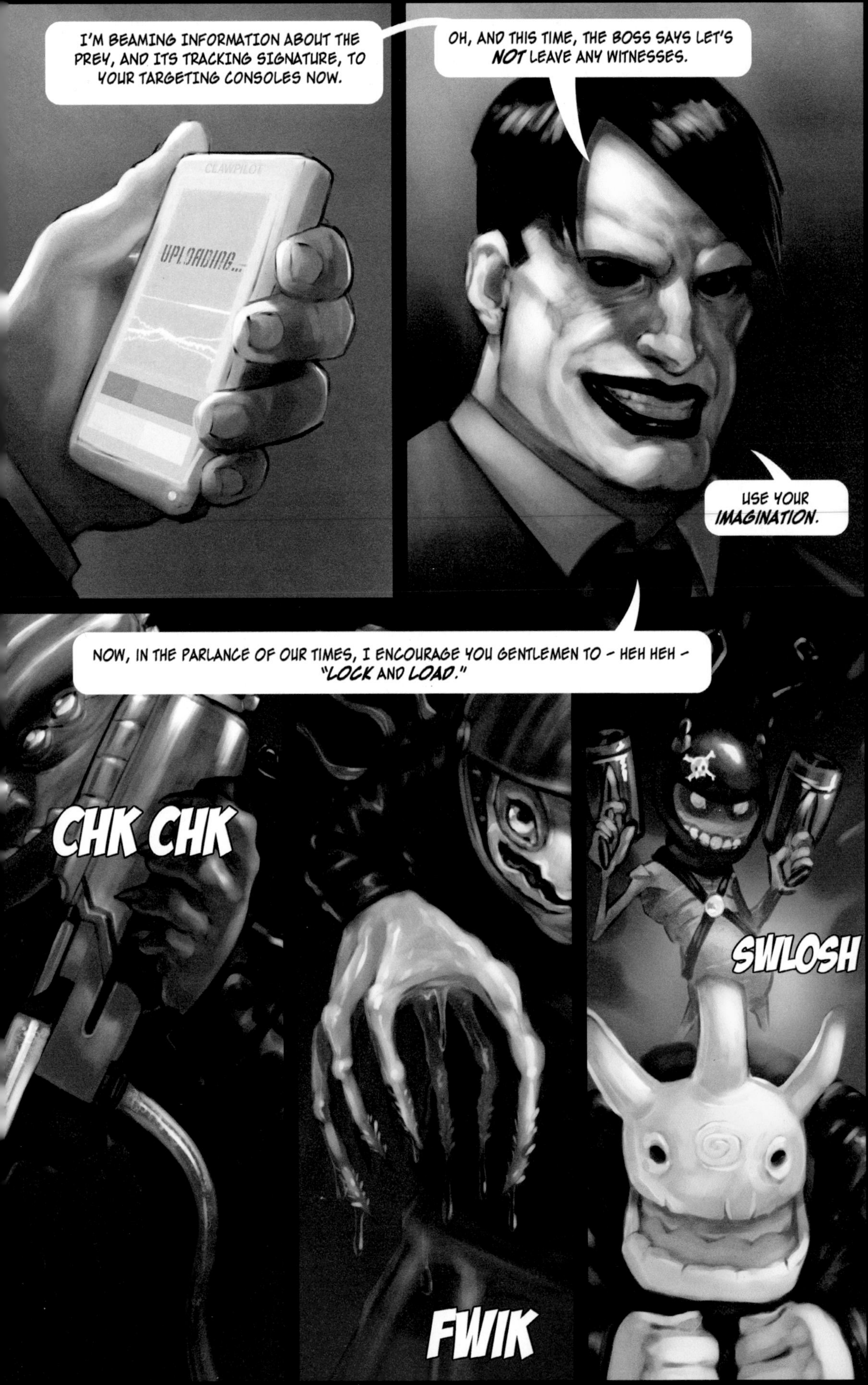
I'M BEAMING INFORMATION ABOUT THE PREY, AND ITS TRACKING SIGNATURE, TO YOUR TARGETING CONSOLES NOW.
CLAWPILOT
UPLOADING...
OH, AND THIS TIME, THE BOSS SAYS LET'S ***NOT*** LEAVE ANY WITNESSES.
USE YOUR ***IMAGINATION.***
NOW, IN THE PARLANCE OF OUR TIMES, I ENCOURAGE YOU GENTLEMEN TO – HEH HEH – "***LOCK*** AND ***LOAD.***"
CHK CHK
FWIK
SWLOSH

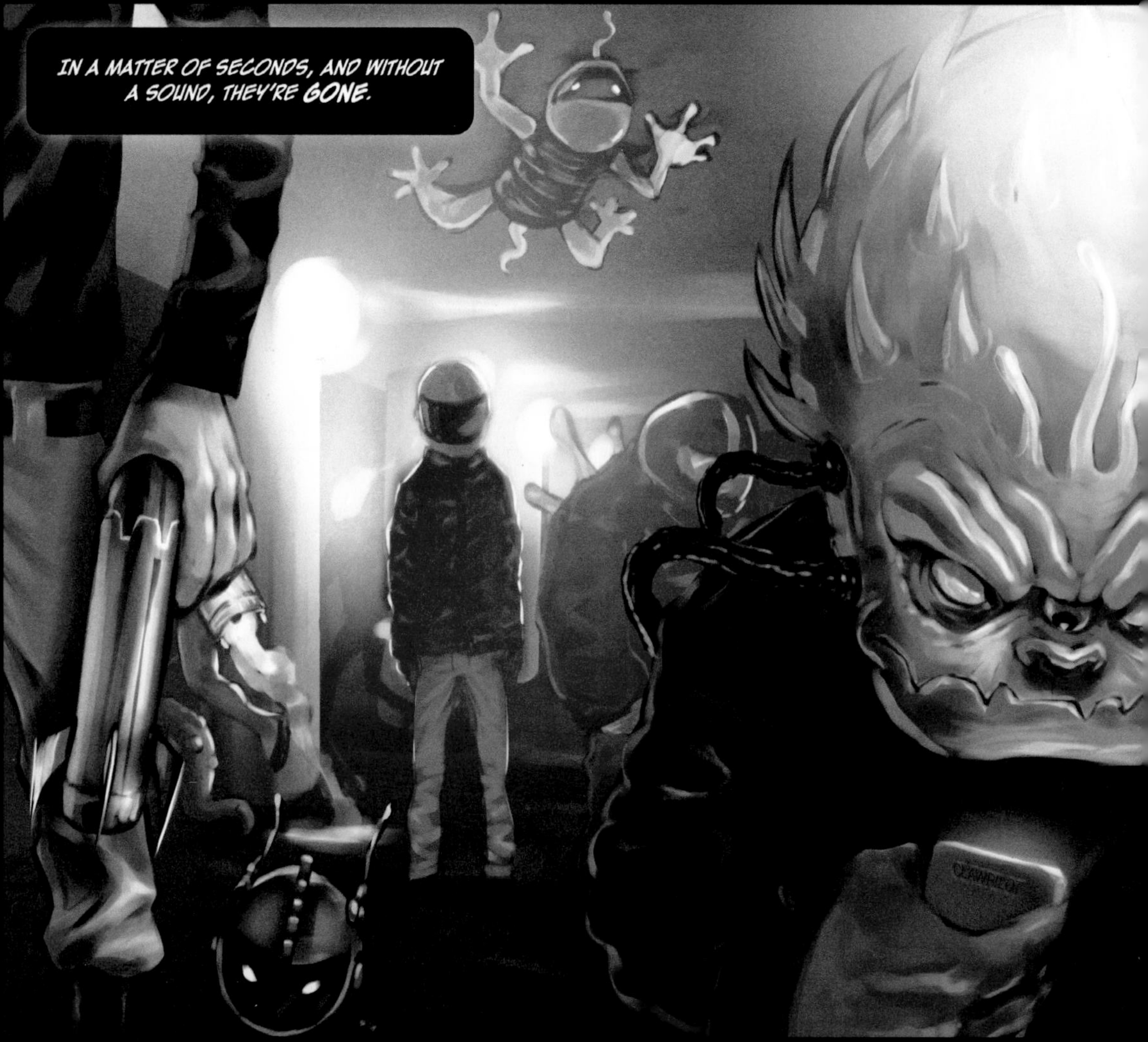
IN A MATTER OF SECONDS, AND WITHOUT A SOUND, THEY'RE **GONE**.

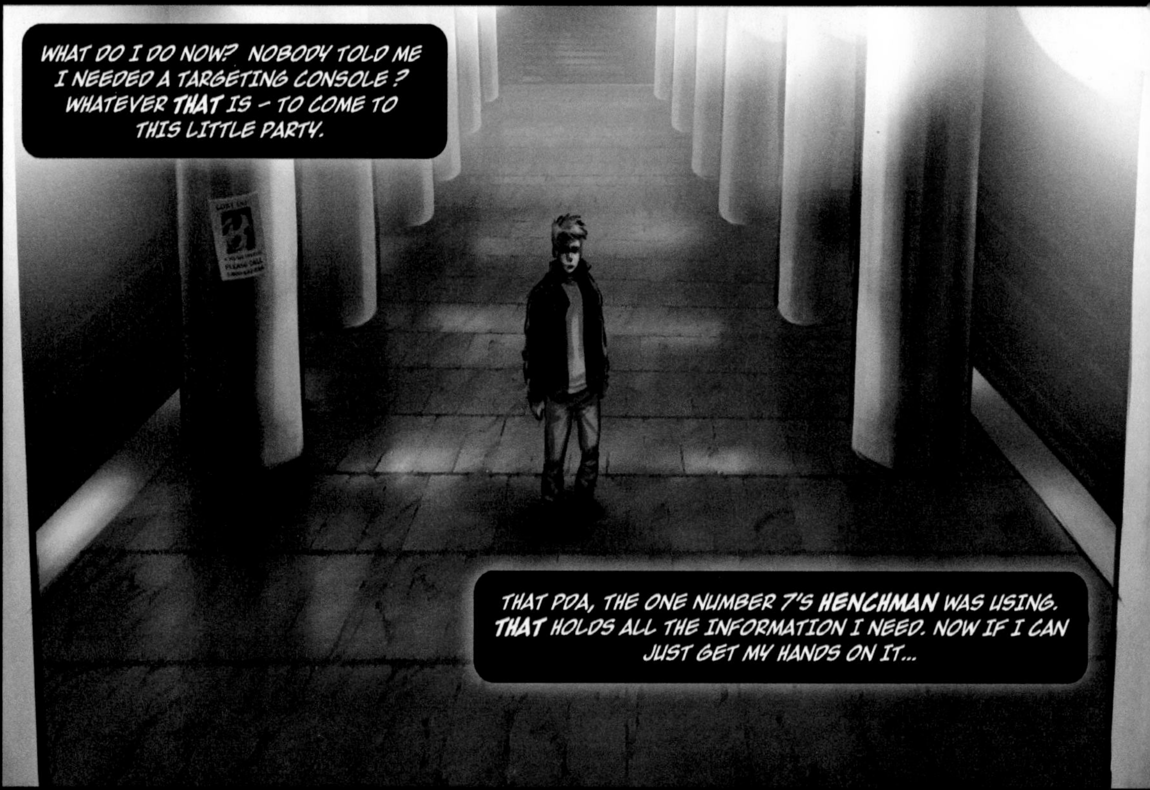
WHAT DO I DO NOW? NOBODY TOLD ME I NEEDED A TARGETING CONSOLE ? WHATEVER **THAT** IS - TO COME TO THIS LITTLE PARTY.
THAT PDA, THE ONE NUMBER 7'S **HENCHMAN** WAS USING. **THAT** HOLDS ALL THE INFORMATION I NEED. NOW IF I CAN JUST GET MY HANDS ON IT...

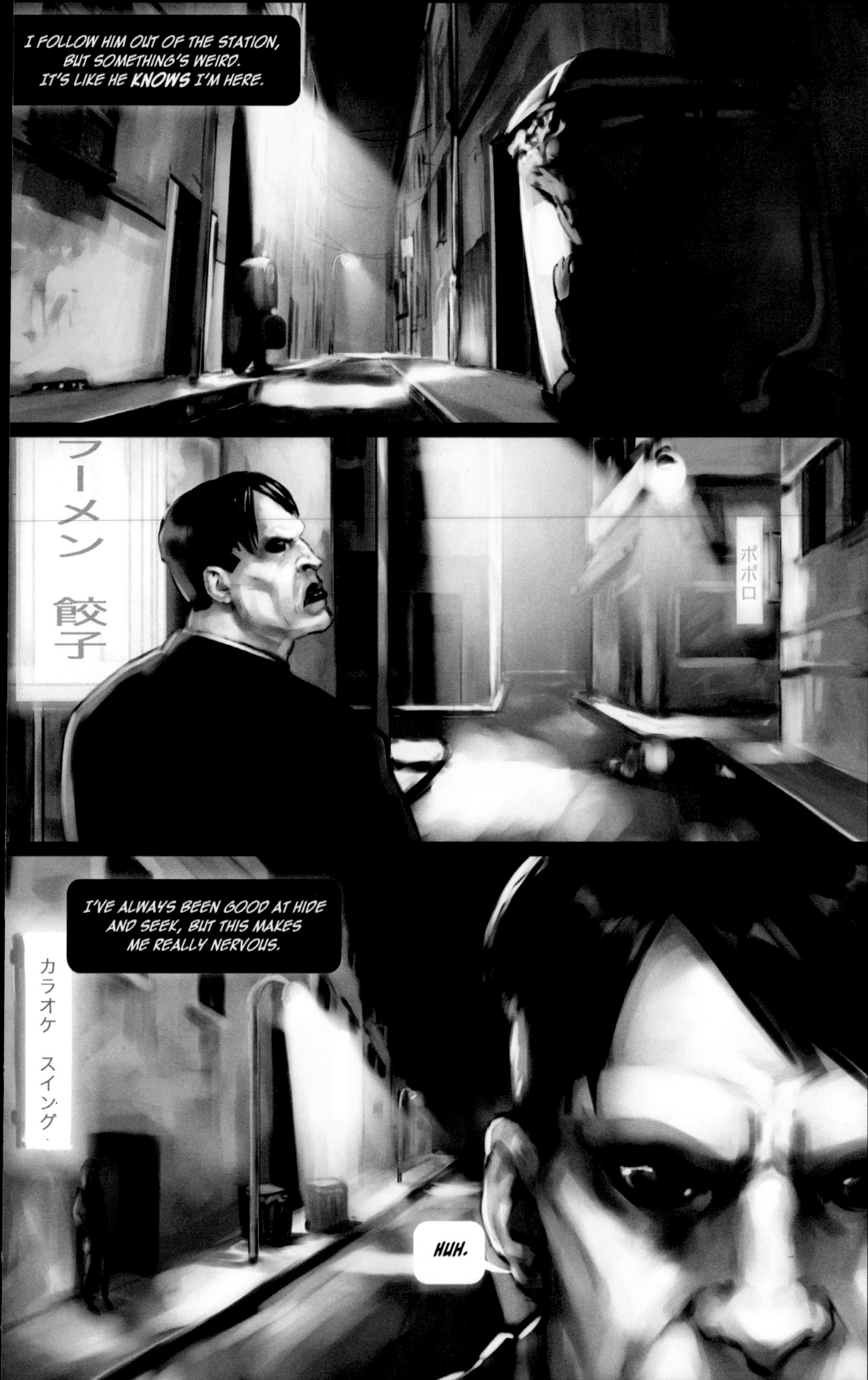

I FOLLOW HIM OUT OF THE STATION, BUT SOMETHING'S WEIRD. IT'S LIKE HE **KNOWS** I'M HERE.
ラーメン 餃子
ポポロ
I'VE ALWAYS BEEN GOOD AT HIDE AND SEEK, BUT THIS MAKES ME REALLY NERVOUS.
カラオケ スイング
HUH.

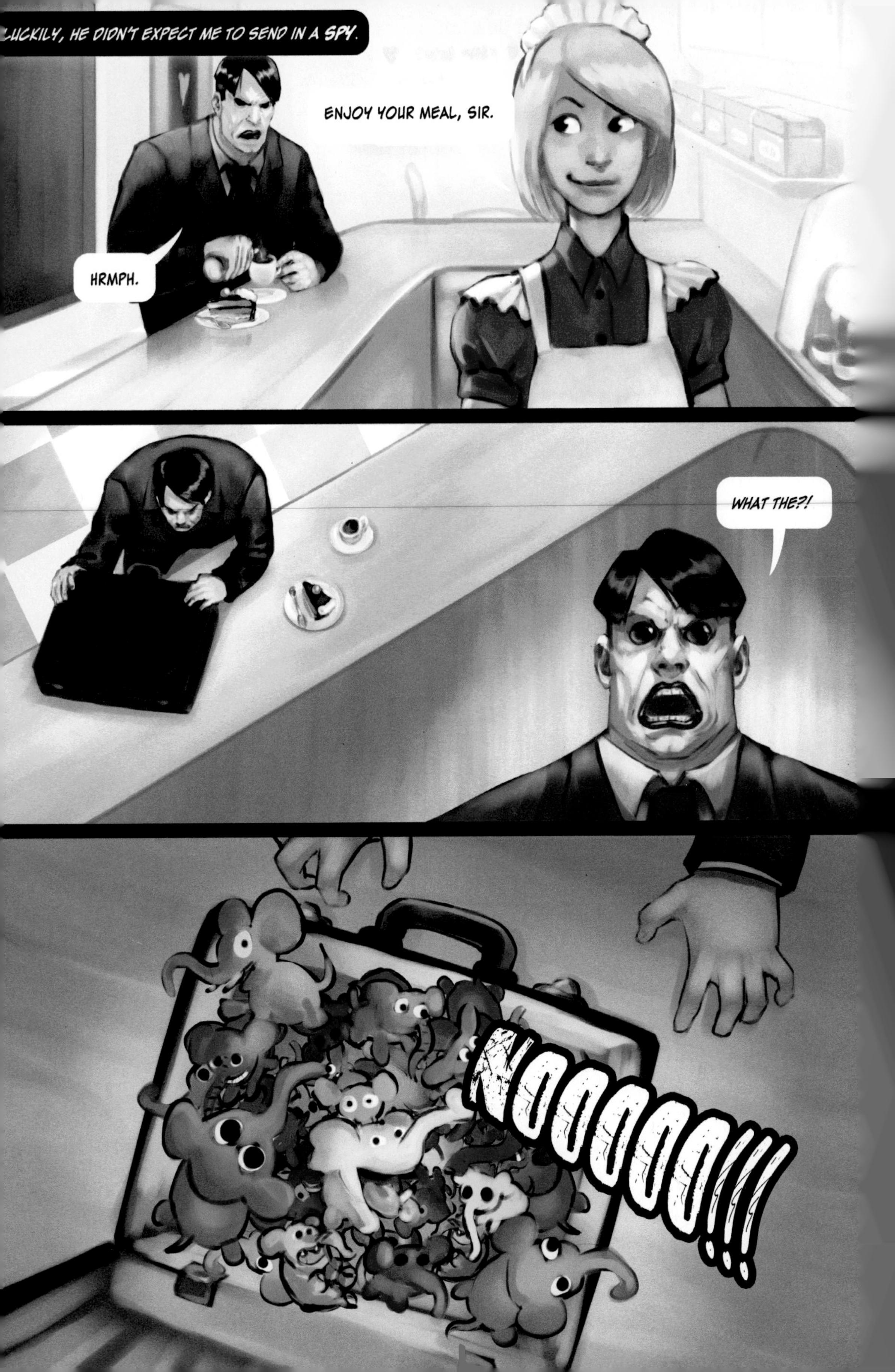
LUCKILY, HE DIDN'T EXPECT ME TO SEND IN A SPY.
ENJOY YOUR MEAL, SIR.
HRMPH.
WHAT THE?!
NOOOOOO!!!

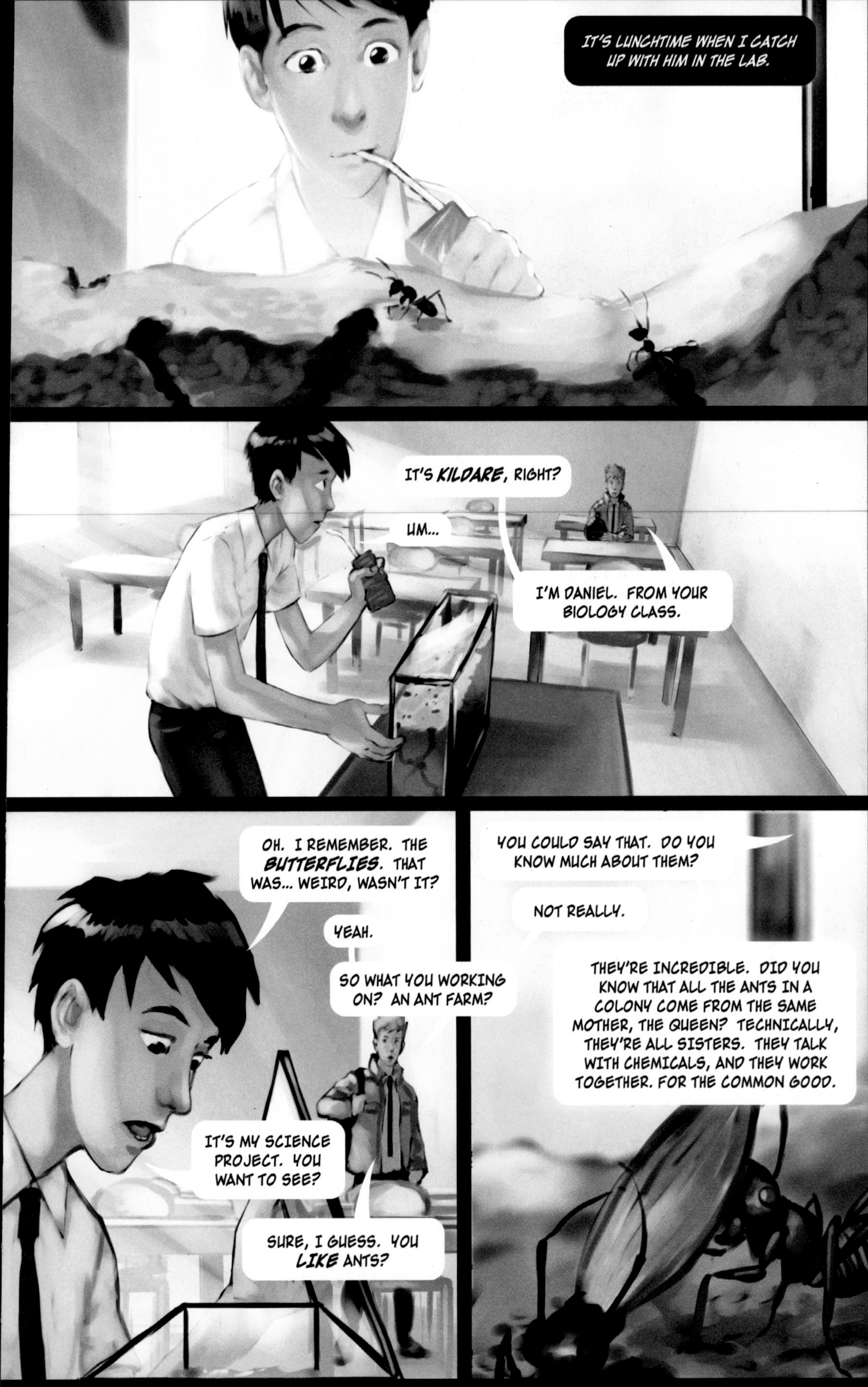

IT'S LUNCHTIME WHEN I CATCH UP WITH HIM IN THE LAB.
IT'S KILDARE, RIGHT?
UM...
I'M DANIEL. FROM YOUR BIOLOGY CLASS.
OH. I REMEMBER. THE BUTTERFLIES. THAT WAS... WEIRD, WASN'T IT?
YEAH.
SO WHAT YOU WORKING ON? AN ANT FARM?
IT'S MY SCIENCE PROJECT. YOU WANT TO SEE?
SURE, I GUESS. YOU LIKE ANTS?
YOU COULD SAY THAT. DO YOU KNOW MUCH ABOUT THEM?
NOT REALLY.
THEY'RE INCREDIBLE. DID YOU KNOW THAT ALL THE ANTS IN A COLONY COME FROM THE SAME MOTHER, THE QUEEN? TECHNICALLY, THEY'RE ALL SISTERS. THEY TALK WITH CHEMICALS, AND THEY WORK TOGETHER. FOR THE COMMON GOOD.

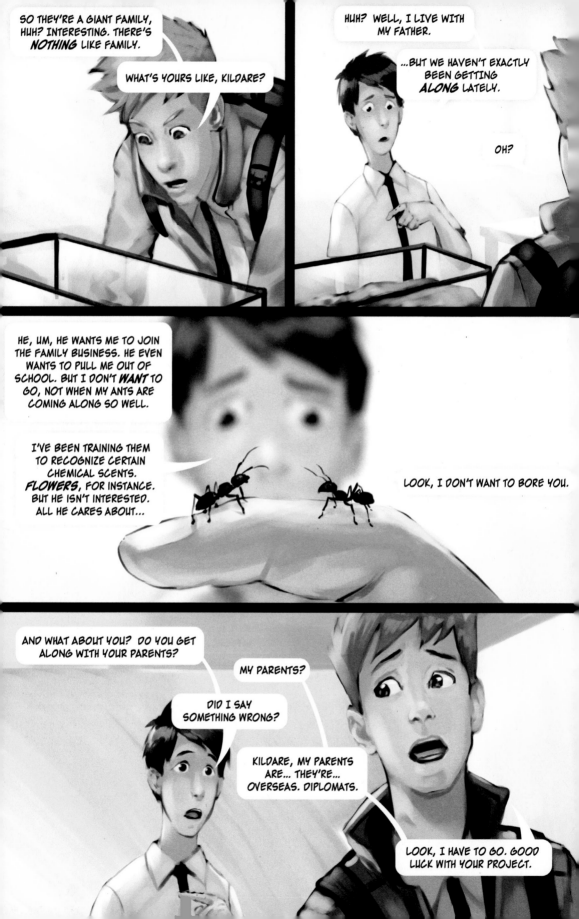

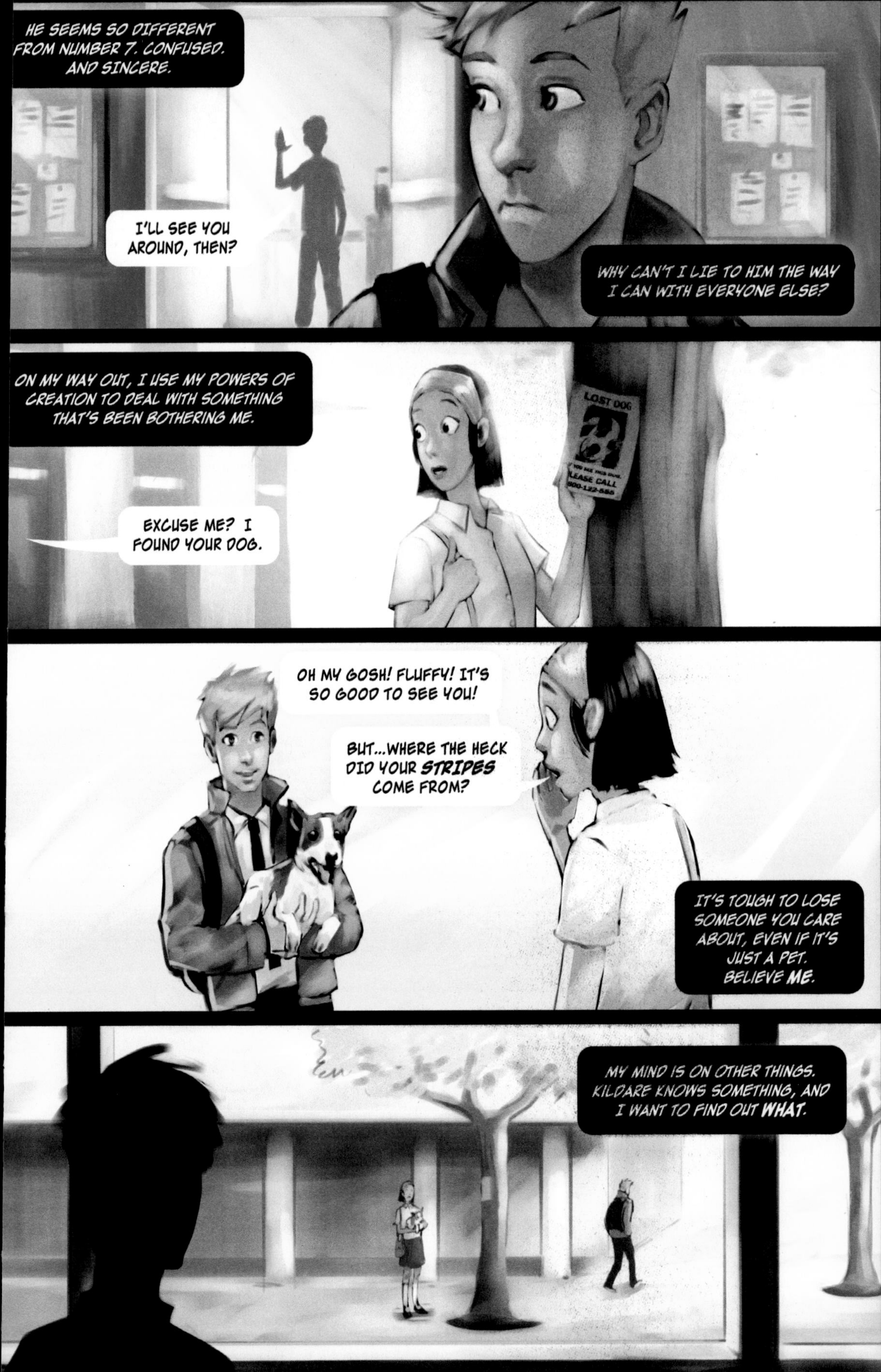
HE SEEMS SO DIFFERENT FROM NUMBER 7. CONFUSED. AND SINCERE.
I'LL SEE YOU AROUND, THEN?
WHY CAN'T I LIE TO HIM THE WAY I CAN WITH EVERYONE ELSE?
ON MY WAY OUT, I USE MY POWERS OF CREATION TO DEAL WITH SOMETHING THAT'S BEEN BOTHERING ME.
LOST DOG
LEASE CALL
EXCUSE ME? I FOUND YOUR DOG.
OH MY GOSH! FLUFFY! IT'S SO GOOD TO SEE YOU!
BUT...WHERE THE HECK DID YOUR STRIPES COME FROM?
IT'S TOUGH TO LOSE SOMEONE YOU CARE ABOUT, EVEN IF IT'S JUST A PET. BELIEVE ME.
MY MIND IS ON OTHER THINGS. KILDARE KNOWS SOMETHING, AND I WANT TO FIND OUT WHAT.

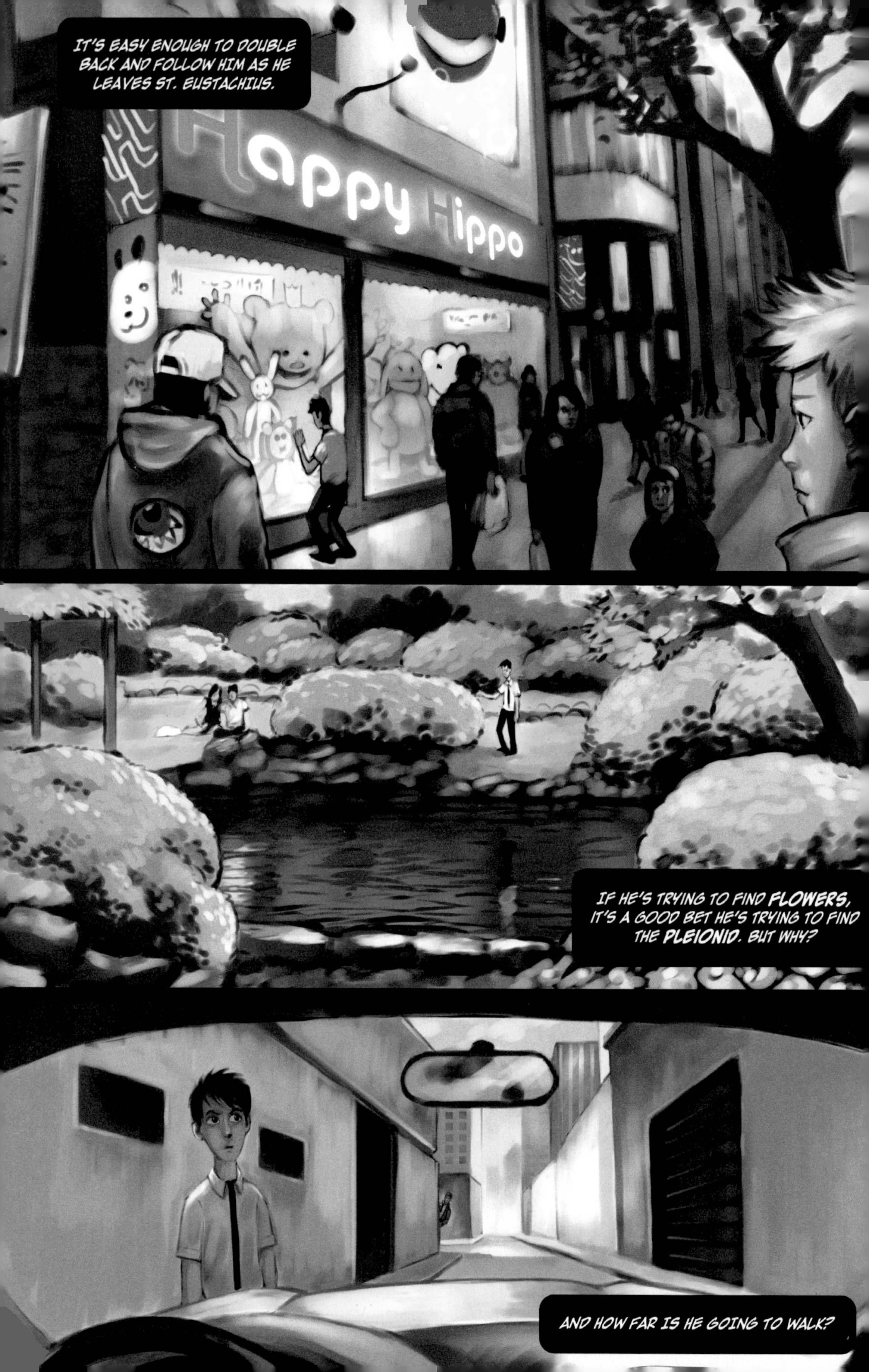
IT'S EASY ENOUGH TO DOUBLE BACK AND FOLLOW HIM AS HE LEAVES ST. EUSTACHIUS.
Happy Hippo
IF HE'S TRYING TO FIND FLOWERS, IT'S A GOOD BET HE'S TRYING TO FIND THE PLEIONID. BUT WHY?
AND HOW FAR IS HE GOING TO WALK?

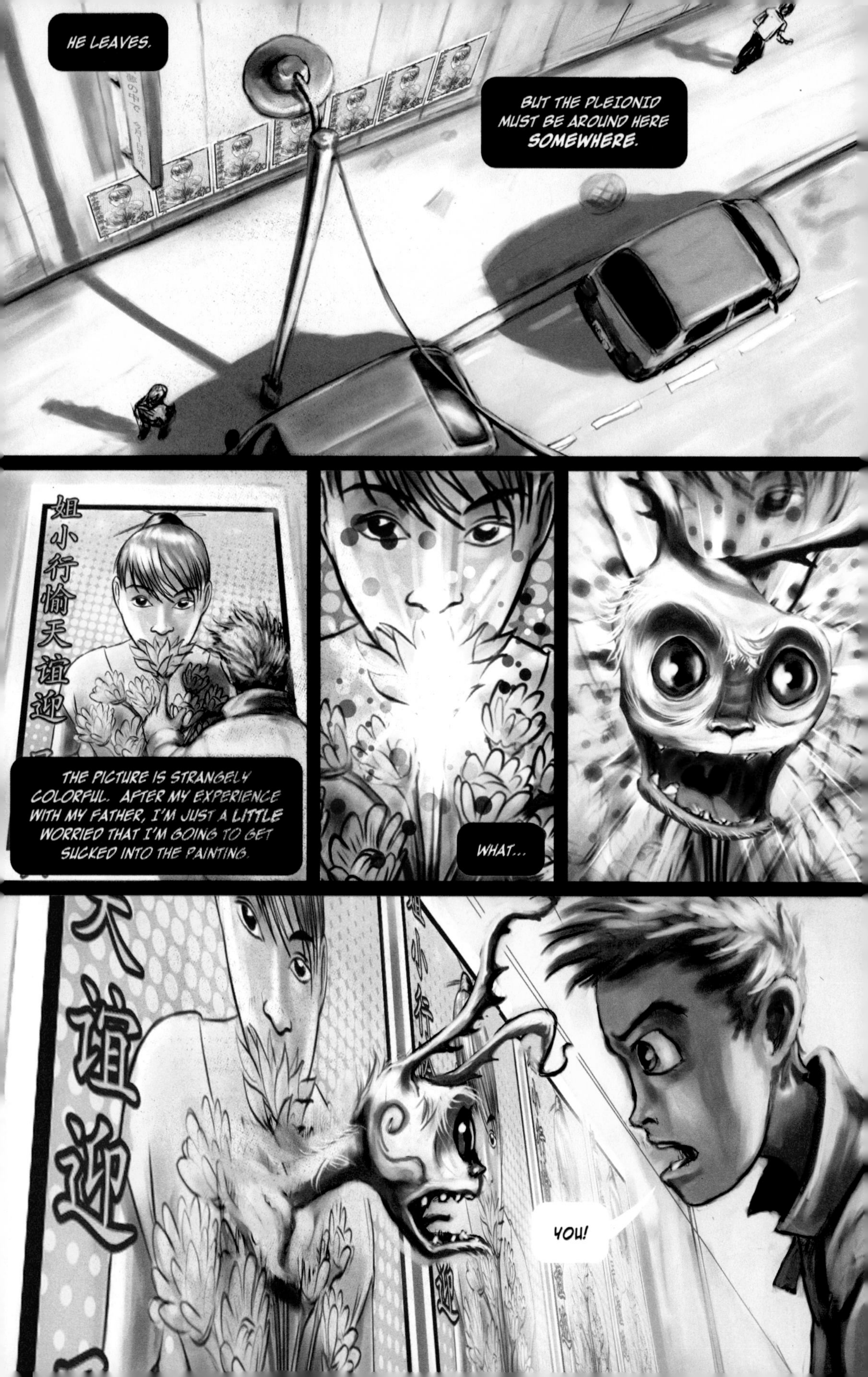
HE LEAVES.
BUT THE PLEIONID MUST BE AROUND HERE SOMEWHERE.
THE PICTURE IS STRANGELY COLORFUL. AFTER MY EXPERIENCE WITH MY FATHER, I'M JUST A LITTLE WORRIED THAT I'M GOING TO GET SUCKED INTO THE PAINTING.
WHAT...
YOU!

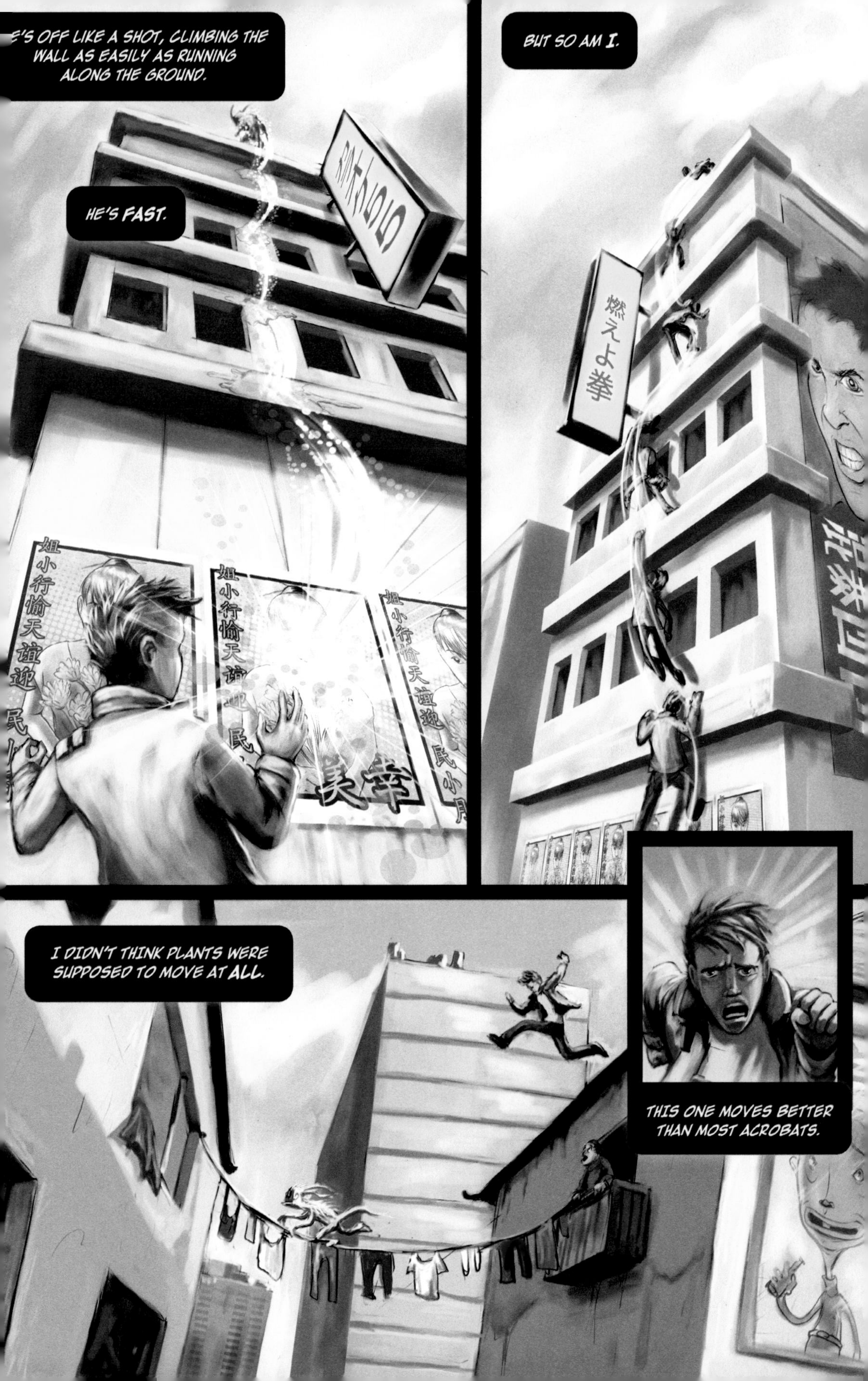
E'S OFF LIKE A SHOT, CLIMBING THE WALL AS EASILY AS RUNNING ALONG THE GROUND.
HE'S FAST.
BUT SO AM I.
燃えよ拳
I DIDN'T THINK PLANTS WERE SUPPOSED TO MOVE AT ALL.
THIS ONE MOVES BETTER THAN MOST ACROBATS.

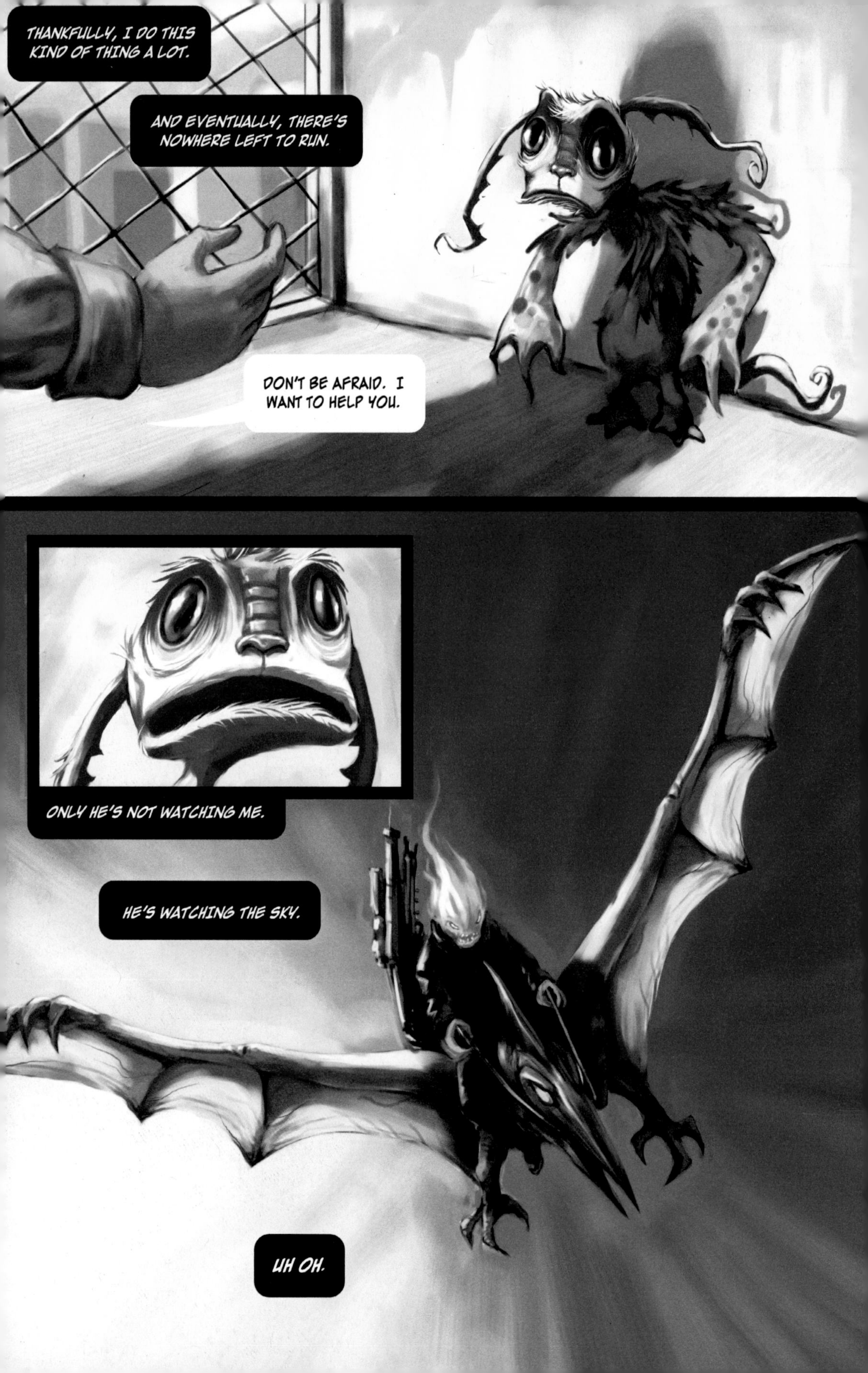
THANKFULLY, I DO THIS KIND OF THING A LOT.
AND EVENTUALLY, THERE'S NOWHERE LEFT TO RUN.
DON'T BE AFRAID. I WANT TO HELP YOU.
ONLY HE'S NOT WATCHING ME.
HE'S WATCHING THE SKY.
UH OH.

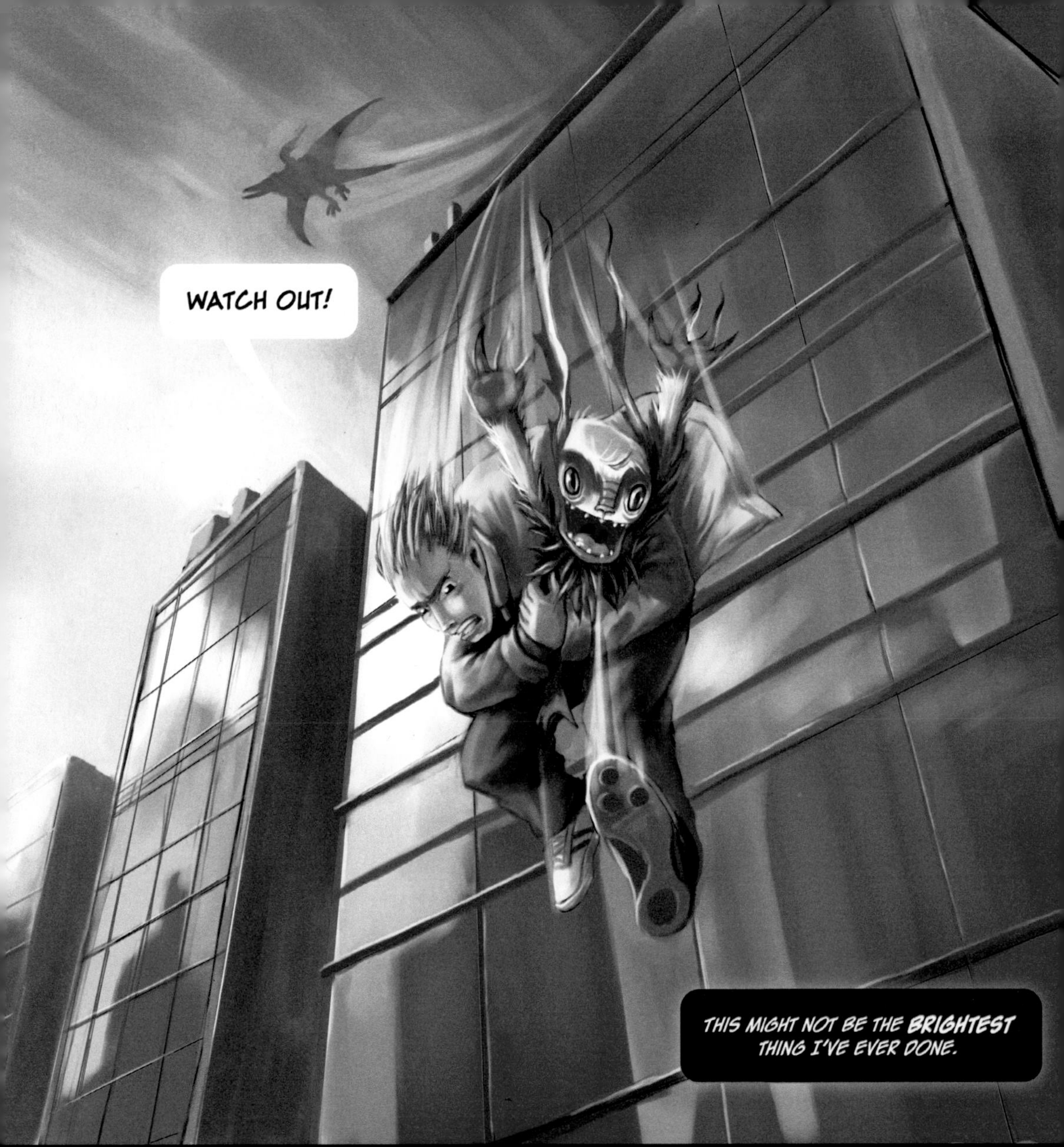
WATCH OUT!
THIS MIGHT NOT BE THE BRIGHTEST THING I'VE EVER DONE.

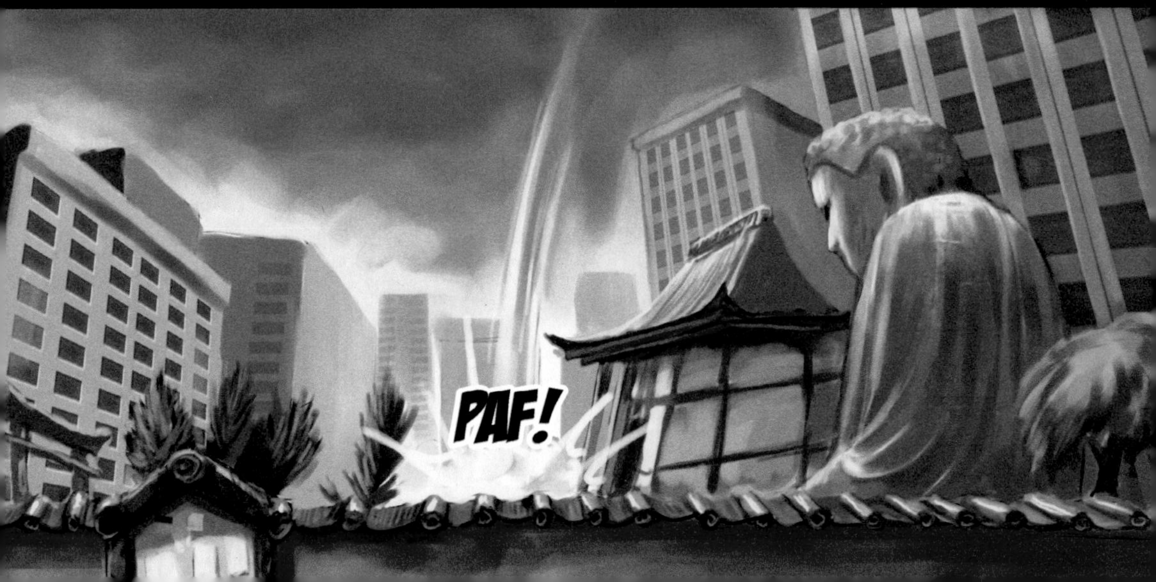
PAF!

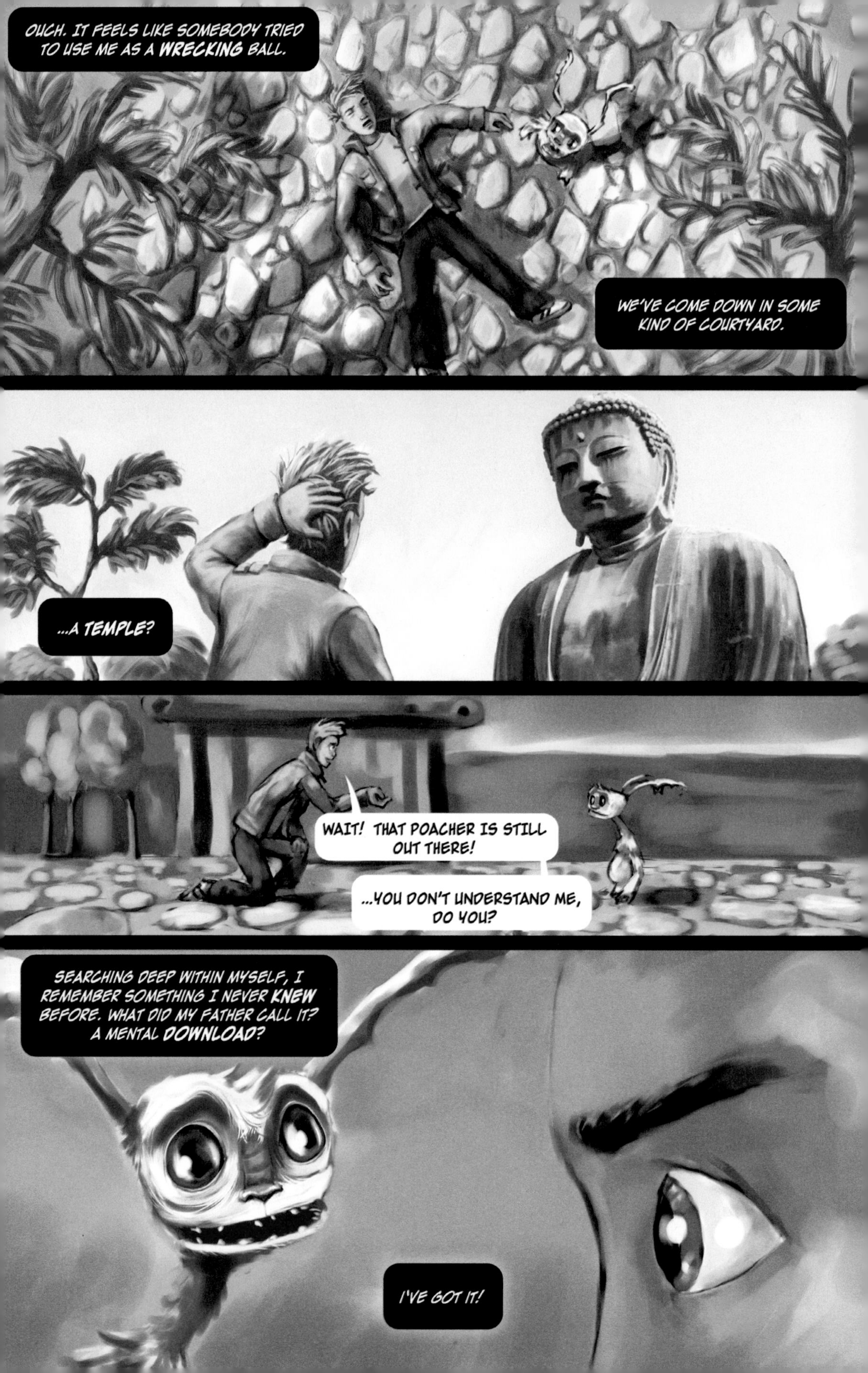
OUCH. IT FEELS LIKE SOMEBODY TRIED TO USE ME AS A WRECKING BALL.
WE'VE COME DOWN IN SOME KIND OF COURTYARD.
...A TEMPLE?
WAIT! THAT POACHER IS STILL OUT THERE!
...YOU DON'T UNDERSTAND ME, DO YOU?
SEARCHING DEEP WITHIN MYSELF, I REMEMBER SOMETHING I NEVER KNEW BEFORE. WHAT DID MY FATHER CALL IT? A MENTAL DOWNLOAD?
I'VE GOT IT!

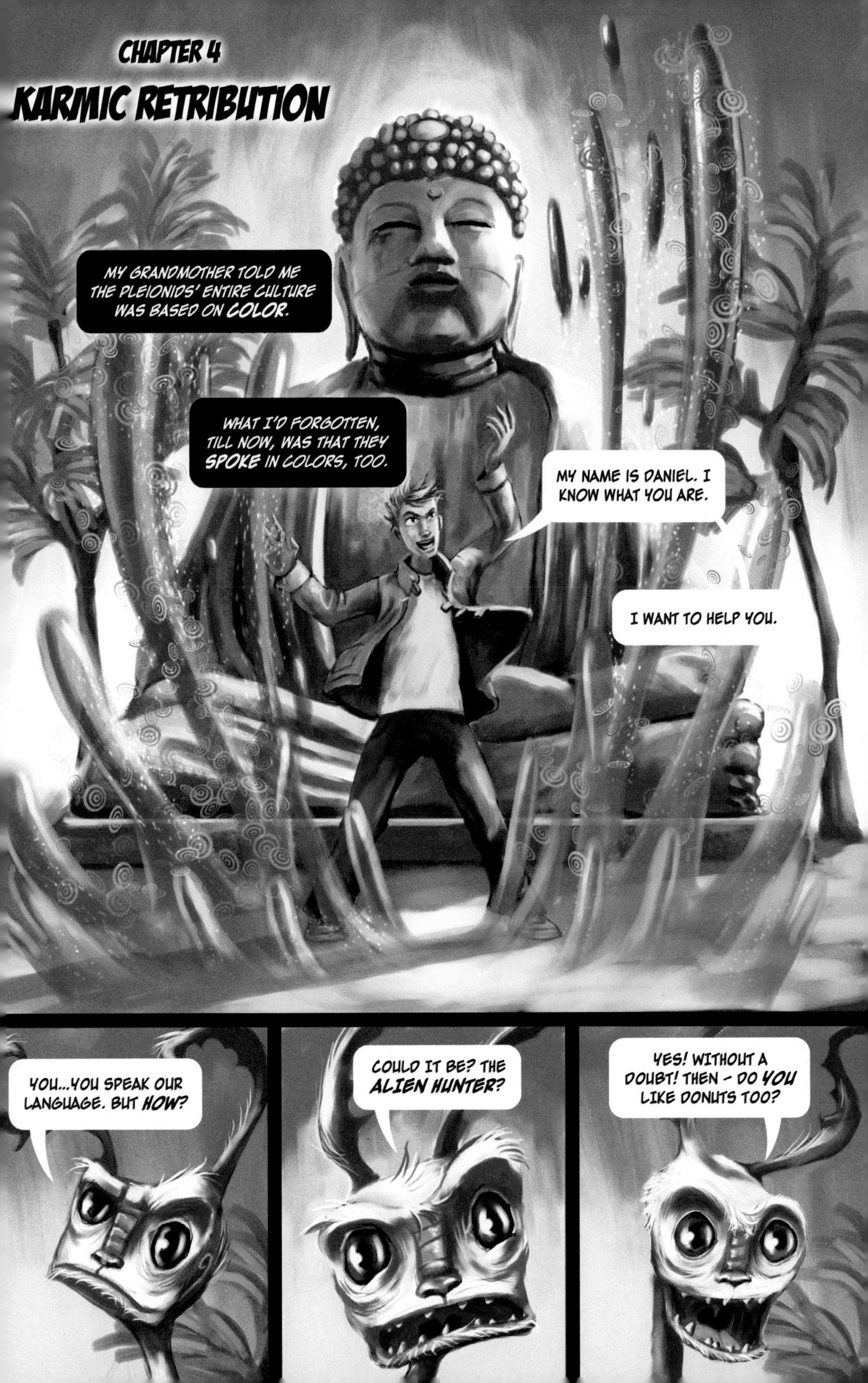
CHAPTER 4
KARMIC RETRIBUTION
MY GRANDMOTHER TOLD ME THE PLEIONIDS' ENTIRE CULTURE WAS BASED ON COLOR.
WHAT I'D FORGOTTEN, TILL NOW, WAS THAT THEY SPOKE IN COLORS, TOO.
MY NAME IS DANIEL. I KNOW WHAT YOU ARE.
I WANT TO HELP YOU.
YOU...YOU SPEAK OUR LANGUAGE. BUT HOW?
COULD IT BE? THE ALIEN HUNTER?
YES! WITHOUT A DOUBT! THEN - DO YOU LIKE DONUTS TOO?

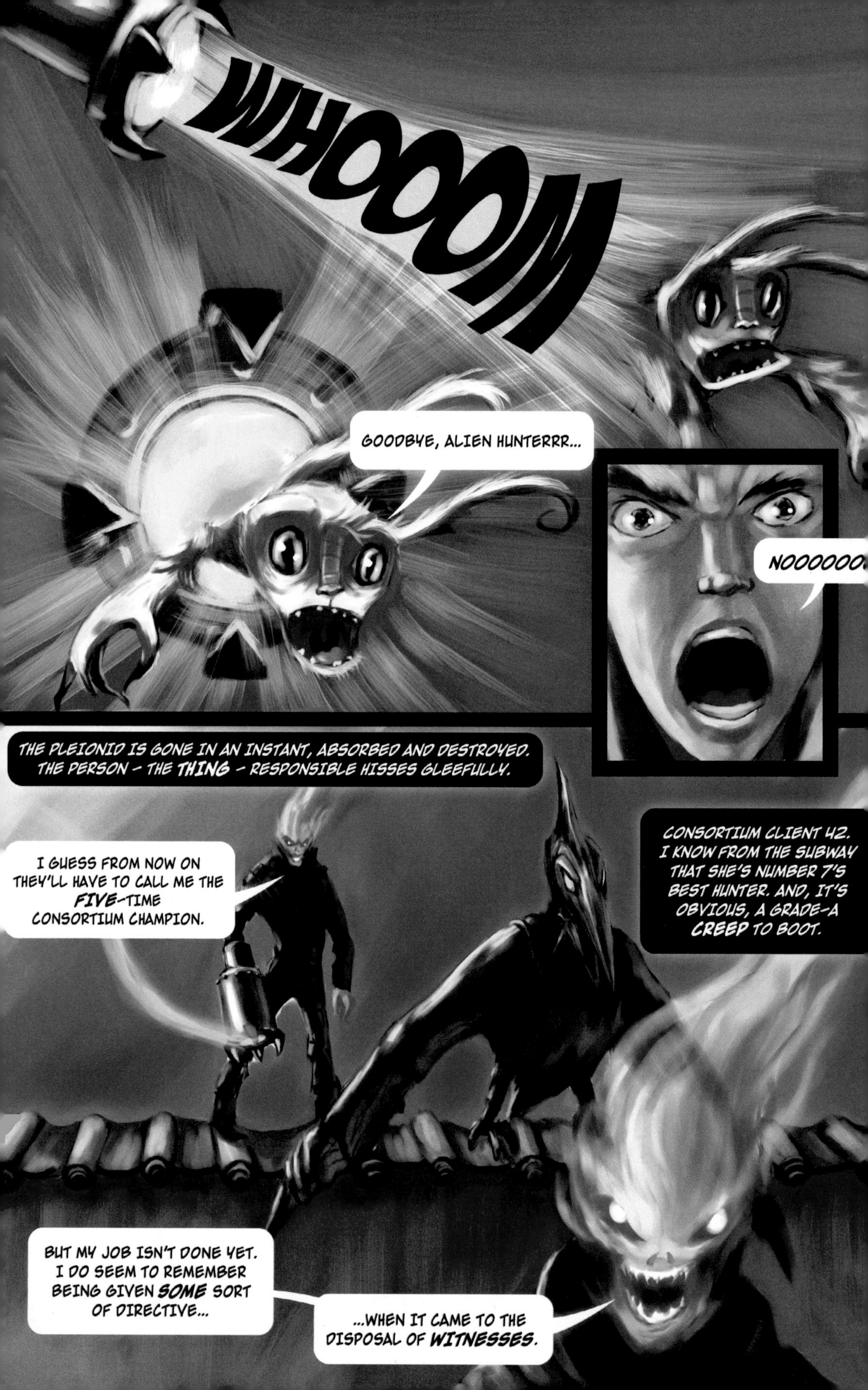
WHOOOM
GOODBYE, ALIEN HUNTERRR...
NOOOOOO
THE PLEIONID IS GONE IN AN INSTANT, ABSORBED AND DESTROYED. THE PERSON - THE THING - RESPONSIBLE HISSES GLEEFULLY.
I GUESS FROM NOW ON THEY'LL HAVE TO CALL ME THE FIVE-TIME CONSORTIUM CHAMPION.
CONSORTIUM CLIENT 42. I KNOW FROM THE SUBWAY THAT SHE'S NUMBER 7'S BEST HUNTER. AND, IT'S OBVIOUS, A GRADE-A CREEP TO BOOT.
BUT MY JOB ISN'T DONE YET. I DO SEEM TO REMEMBER BEING GIVEN SOME SORT OF DIRECTIVE...
...WHEN IT CAME TO THE DISPOSAL OF WITNESSES.

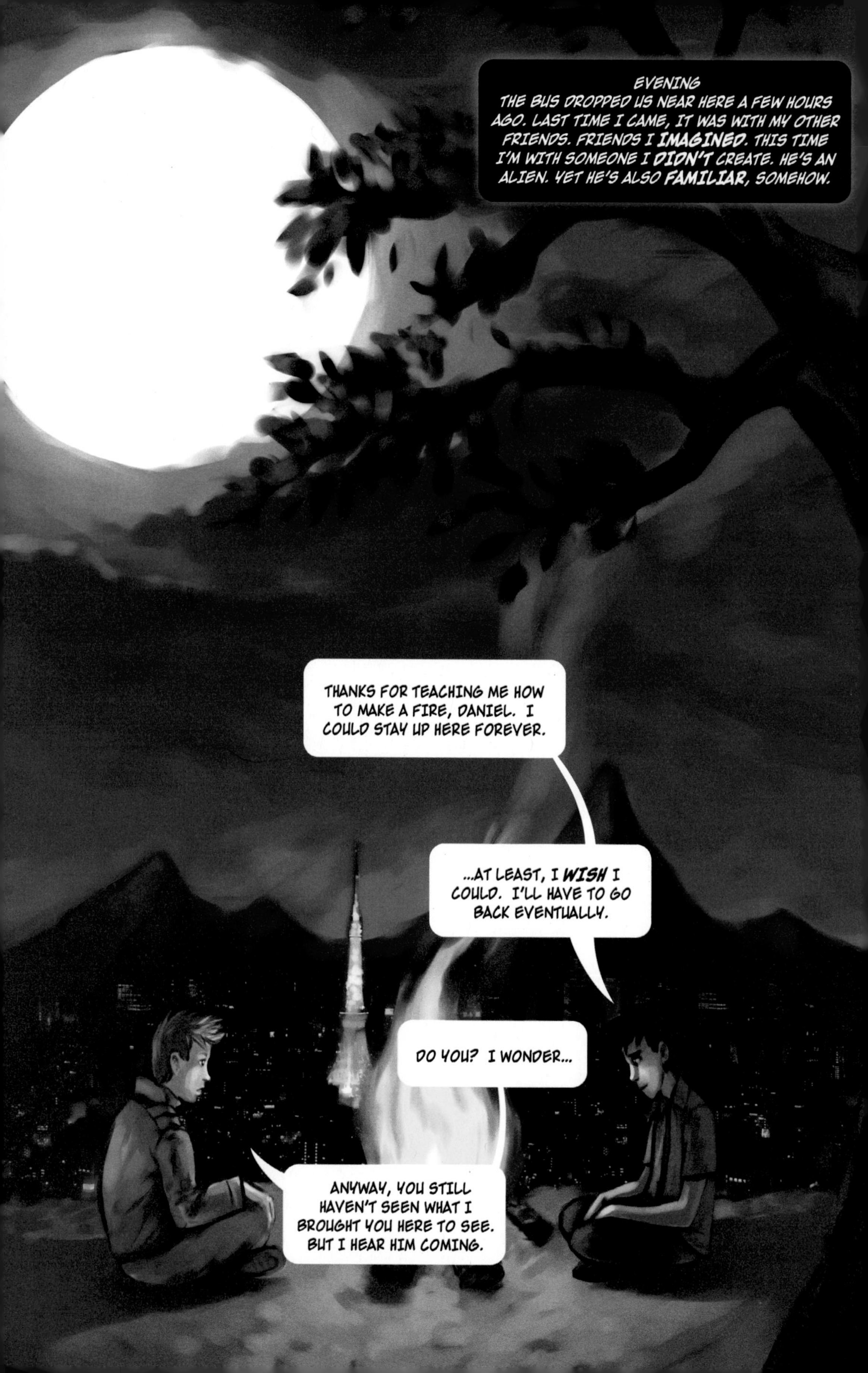
EVENING
THE BUS DROPPED US NEAR HERE A FEW HOURS AGO. LAST TIME I CAME, IT WAS WITH MY OTHER FRIENDS. FRIENDS I IMAGINED. THIS TIME I'M WITH SOMEONE I DIDN'T CREATE. HE'S AN ALIEN. YET HE'S ALSO FAMILIAR, SOMEHOW.
THANKS FOR TEACHING ME HOW TO MAKE A FIRE, DANIEL. I COULD STAY UP HERE FOREVER.
...AT LEAST, I WISH I COULD. I'LL HAVE TO GO BACK EVENTUALLY.
DO YOU? I WONDER...
ANYWAY, YOU STILL HAVEN'T SEEN WHAT I BROUGHT YOU HERE TO SEE. BUT I HEAR HIM COMING.

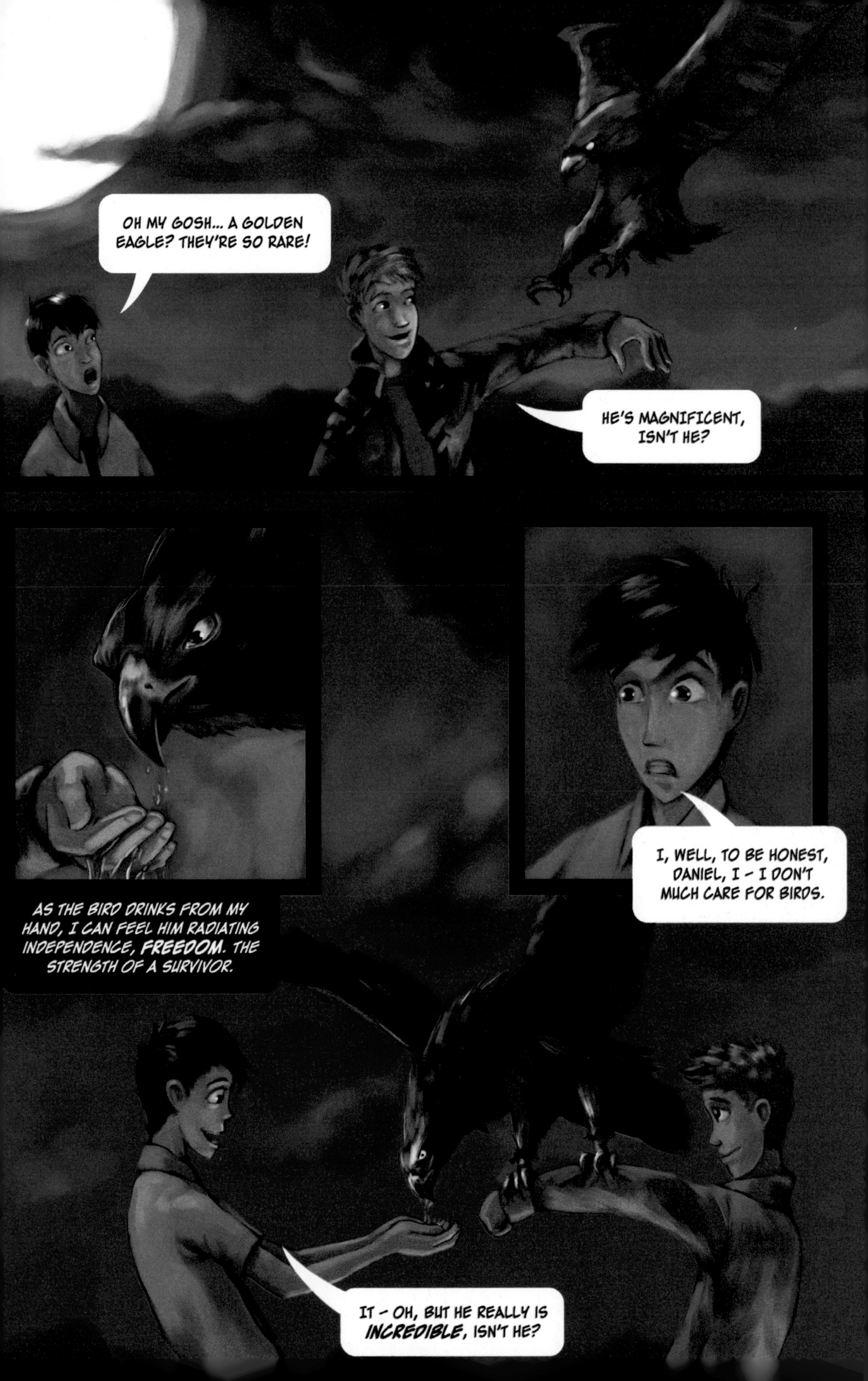
OH MY GOSH... A GOLDEN EAGLE? THEY'RE SO RARE!
HE'S MAGNIFICENT, ISN'T HE?
AS THE BIRD DRINKS FROM MY HAND, I CAN FEEL HIM RADIATING INDEPENDENCE, **FREEDOM**. THE STRENGTH OF A SURVIVOR.
I, WELL, TO BE HONEST, DANIEL, I - I DON'T MUCH CARE FOR BIRDS.
IT - OH, BUT HE REALLY IS ***INCREDIBLE***, ISN'T HE?

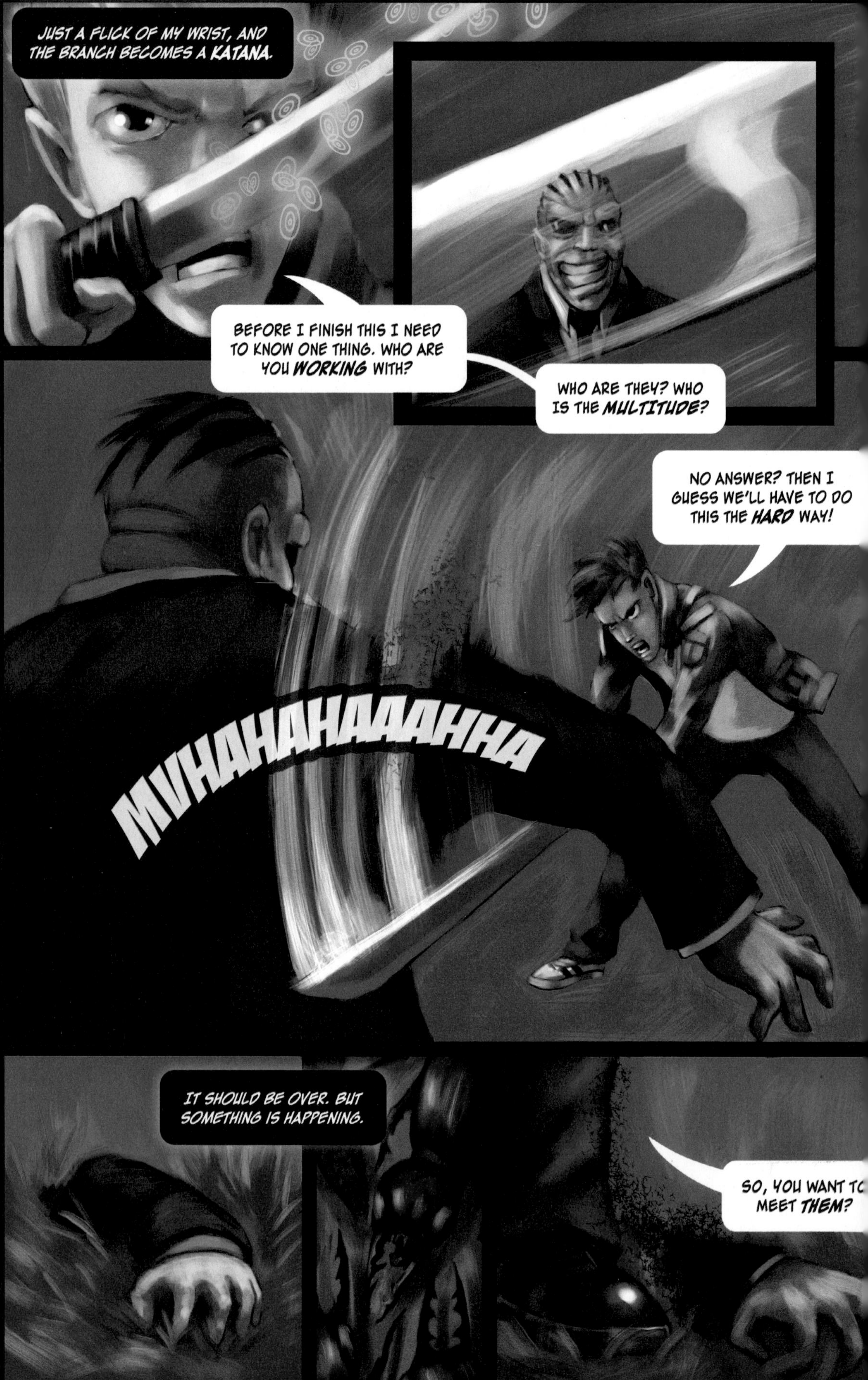
JUST A FLICK OF MY WRIST, AND THE BRANCH BECOMES A KATANA.
BEFORE I FINISH THIS I NEED TO KNOW ONE THING. WHO ARE YOU WORKING WITH?
WHO ARE THEY? WHO IS THE MULTITUDE?
NO ANSWER? THEN I GUESS WE'LL HAVE TO DO THIS THE HARD WAY!
MVHAHAHAAAHHA
IT SHOULD BE OVER. BUT SOMETHING IS HAPPENING.
SO, YOU WANT TO MEET THEM?

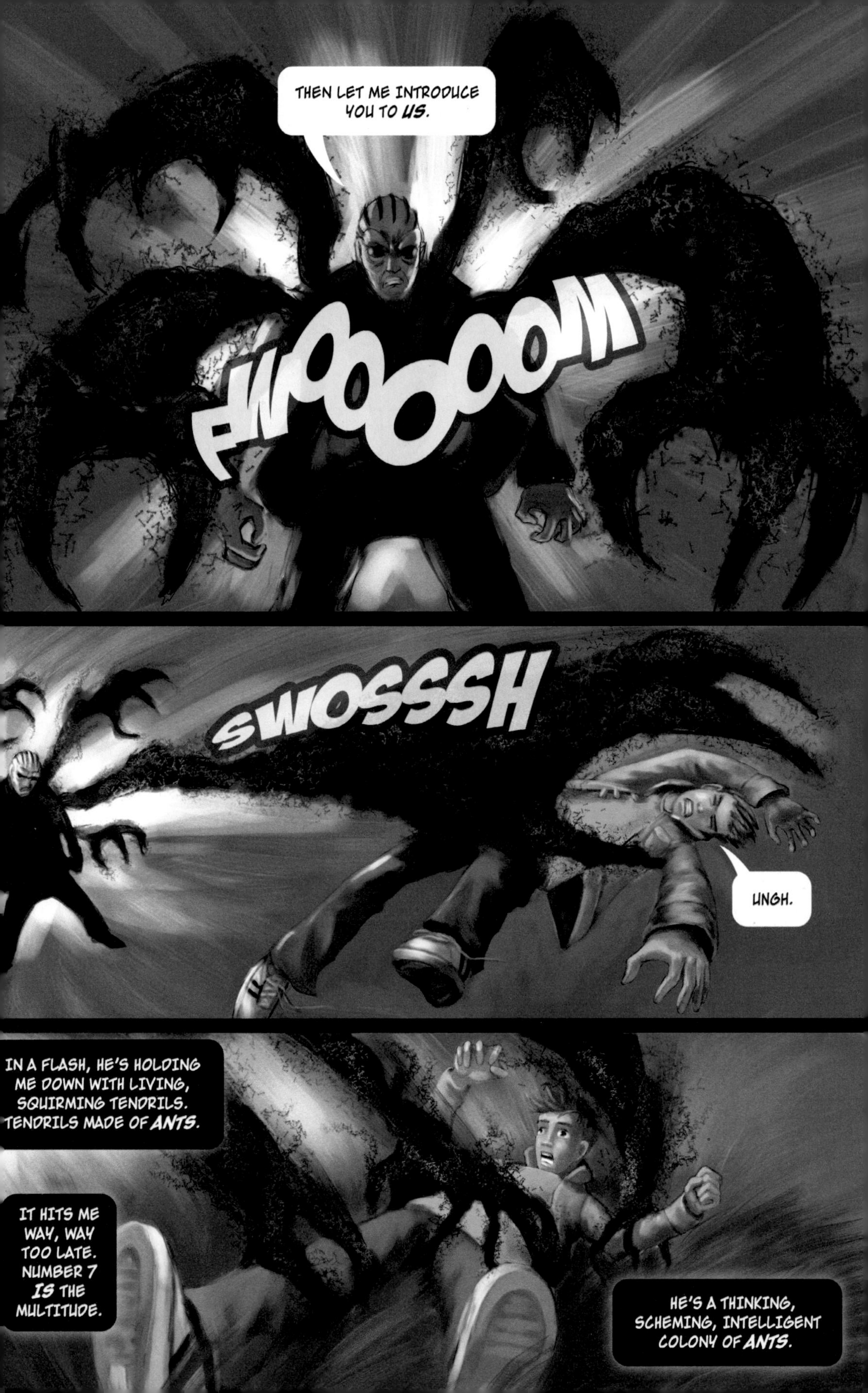
THEN LET ME INTRODUCE YOU TO *US*.
FWOOOOOM
SWOSSSH
UNGH.
IN A FLASH, HE'S HOLDING ME DOWN WITH LIVING, SQUIRMING TENDRILS. TENDRILS MADE OF *ANTS*.
IT HITS ME WAY, WAY TOO LATE. NUMBER 7 *IS* THE MULTITUDE.
HE'S A THINKING, SCHEMING, INTELLIGENT COLONY OF *ANTS*.

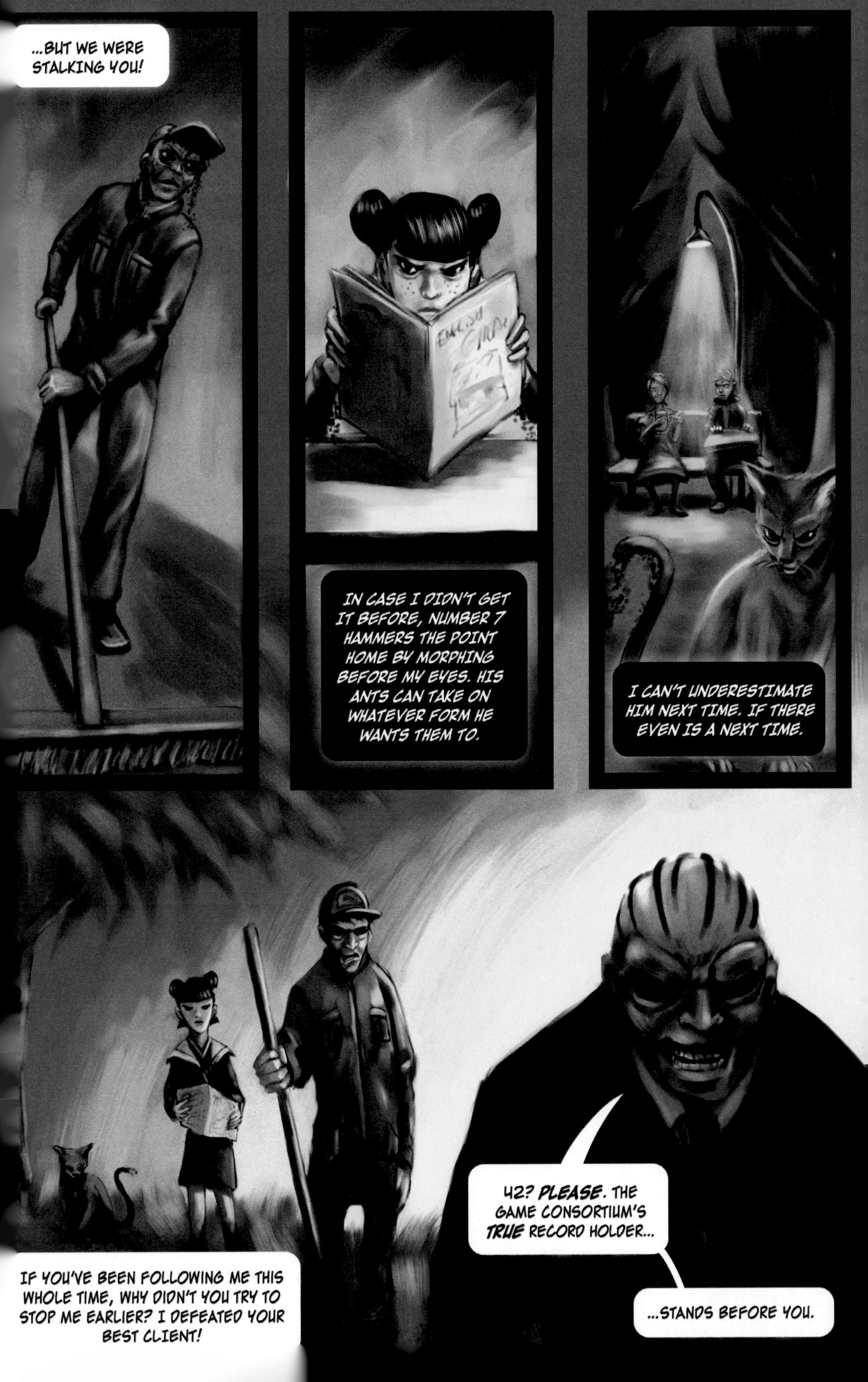
...BUT WE WERE STALKING YOU!
IN CASE I DIDN'T GET IT BEFORE, NUMBER 7 HAMMERS THE POINT HOME BY MORPHING BEFORE MY EYES. HIS ANTS CAN TAKE ON WHATEVER FORM HE WANTS THEM TO.
I CAN'T UNDERESTIMATE HIM NEXT TIME. IF THERE EVEN IS A NEXT TIME.
IF YOU'VE BEEN FOLLOWING ME THIS WHOLE TIME, WHY DIDN'T YOU TRY TO STOP ME EARLIER? I DEFEATED YOUR BEST CLIENT!
42? PLEASE. THE GAME CONSORTIUM'S TRUE RECORD HOLDER...
...STANDS BEFORE YOU.

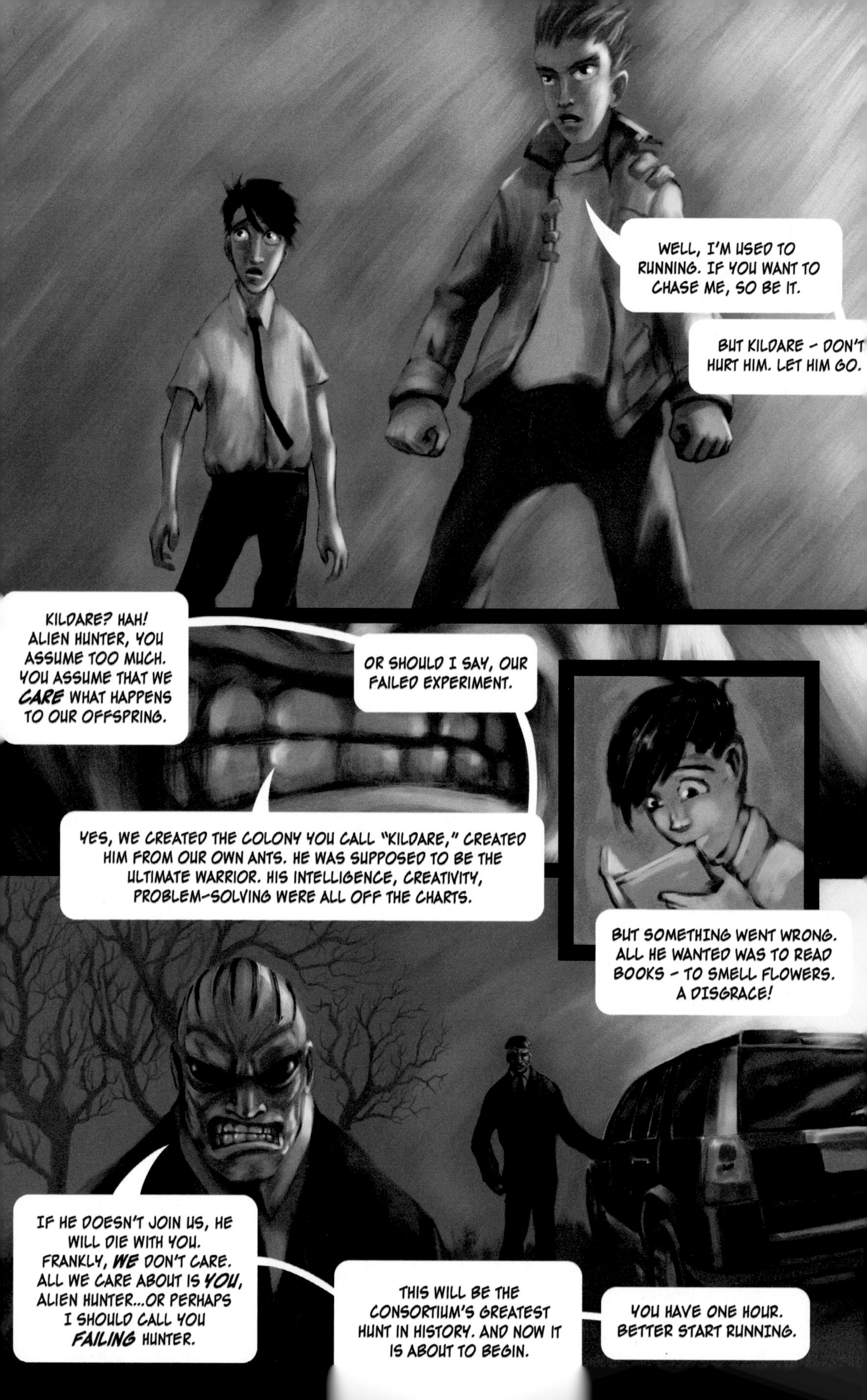
WELL, I'M USED TO RUNNING. IF YOU WANT TO CHASE ME, SO BE IT.
BUT KILDARE - DON'T HURT HIM. LET HIM GO.
KILDARE? HAH! ALIEN HUNTER, YOU ASSUME TOO MUCH. YOU ASSUME THAT WE CARE WHAT HAPPENS TO OUR OFFSPRING.
OR SHOULD I SAY, OUR FAILED EXPERIMENT.
YES, WE CREATED THE COLONY YOU CALL "KILDARE," CREATED HIM FROM OUR OWN ANTS. HE WAS SUPPOSED TO BE THE ULTIMATE WARRIOR. HIS INTELLIGENCE, CREATIVITY, PROBLEM-SOLVING WERE ALL OFF THE CHARTS.
BUT SOMETHING WENT WRONG. ALL HE WANTED WAS TO READ BOOKS - TO SMELL FLOWERS. A DISGRACE!
IF HE DOESN'T JOIN US, HE WILL DIE WITH YOU. FRANKLY, WE DON'T CARE. ALL WE CARE ABOUT IS YOU, ALIEN HUNTER...OR PERHAPS I SHOULD CALL YOU FAILING HUNTER.
THIS WILL BE THE CONSORTIUM'S GREATEST HUNT IN HISTORY. AND NOW IT IS ABOUT TO BEGIN.
YOU HAVE ONE HOUR. BETTER START RUNNING.

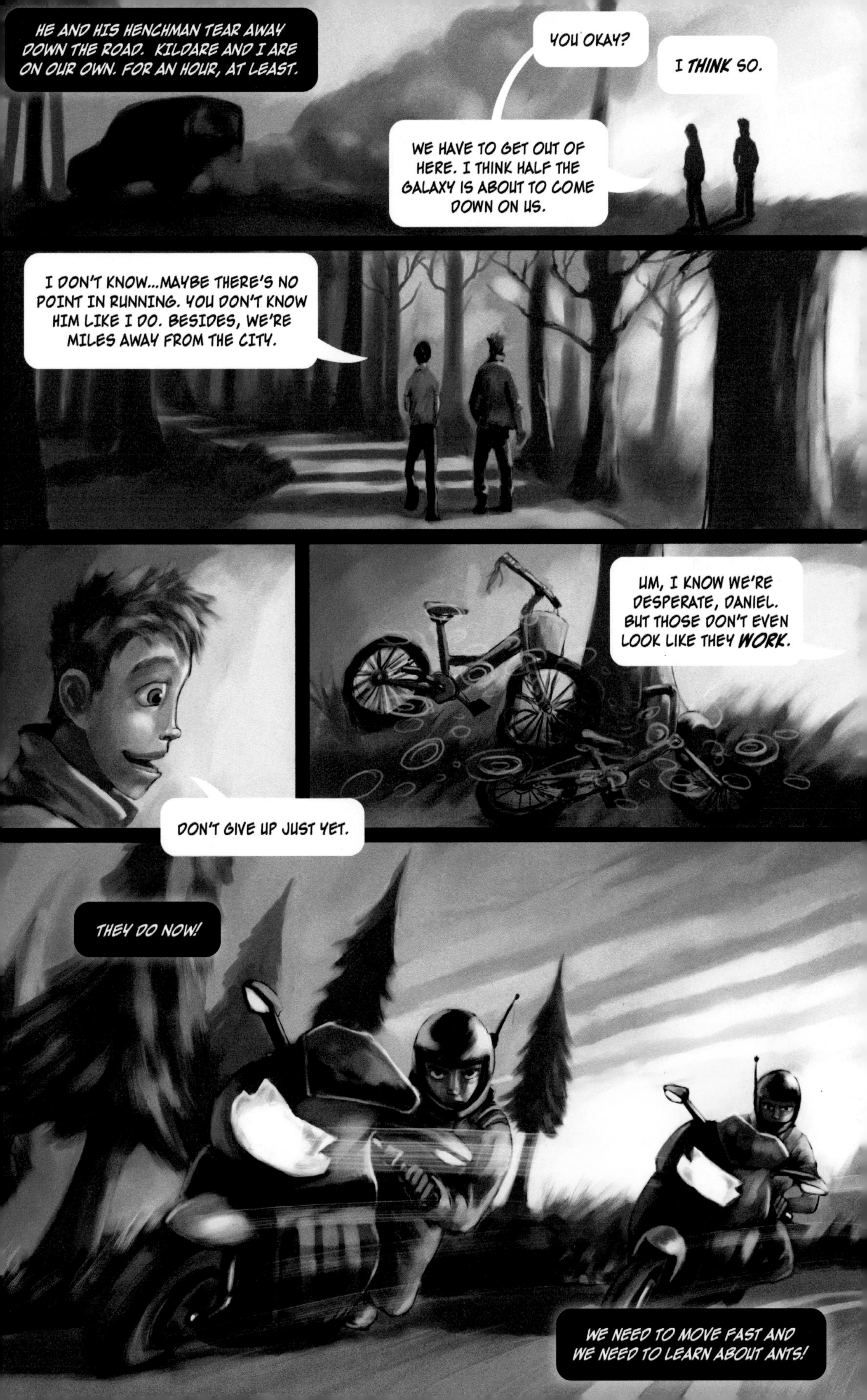
HE AND HIS HENCHMAN TEAR AWAY DOWN THE ROAD. KILDARE AND I ARE ON OUR OWN. FOR AN HOUR, AT LEAST.
YOU OKAY?
I THINK SO.
WE HAVE TO GET OUT OF HERE. I THINK HALF THE GALAXY IS ABOUT TO COME DOWN ON US.
I DON'T KNOW...MAYBE THERE'S NO POINT IN RUNNING. YOU DON'T KNOW HIM LIKE I DO. BESIDES, WE'RE MILES AWAY FROM THE CITY.
DON'T GIVE UP JUST YET.
UM, I KNOW WE'RE DESPERATE, DANIEL. BUT THOSE DON'T EVEN LOOK LIKE THEY WORK.
THEY DO NOW!
WE NEED TO MOVE FAST AND WE NEED TO LEARN ABOUT ANTS!

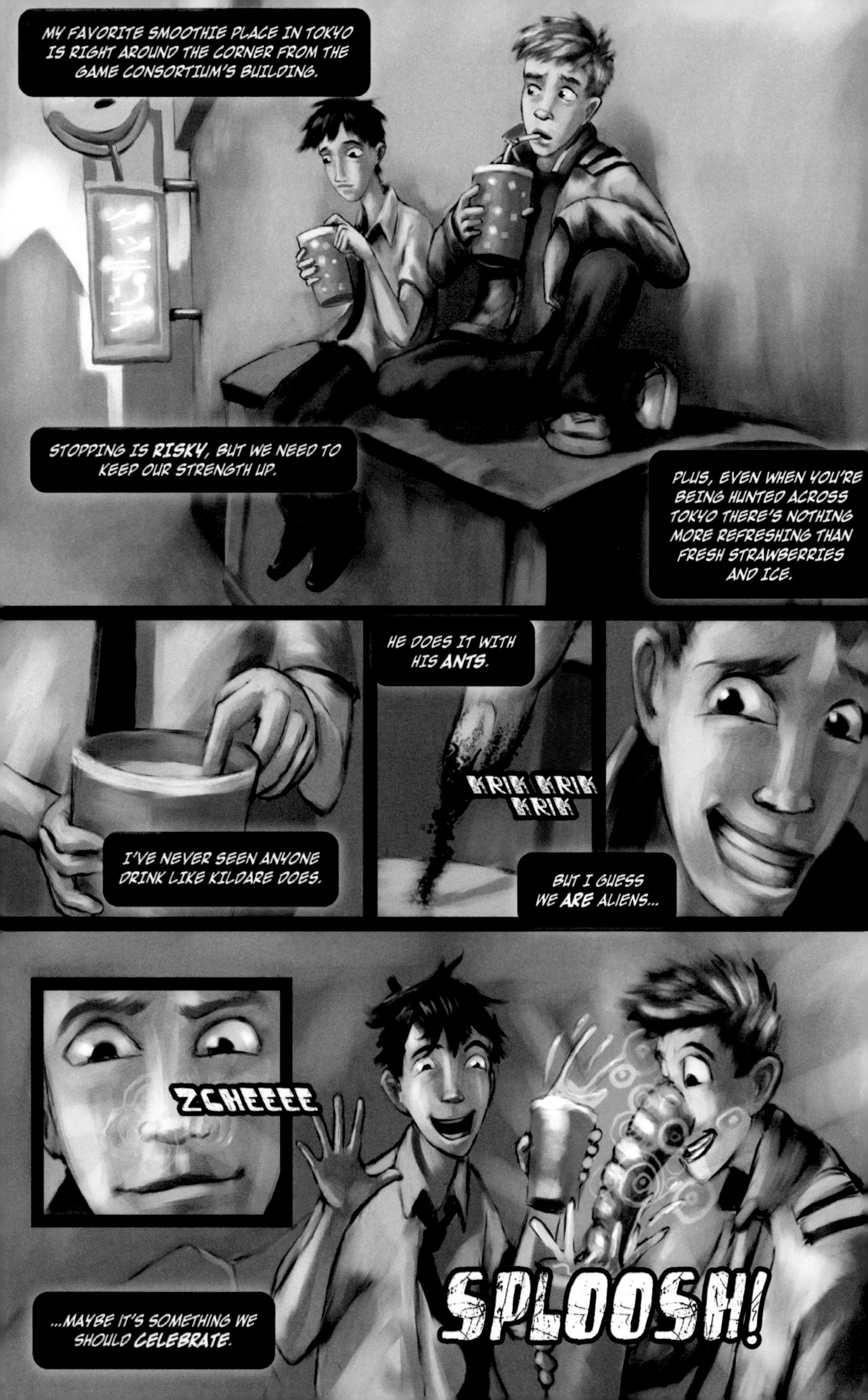
MY FAVORITE SMOOTHIE PLACE IN TOKYO IS RIGHT AROUND THE CORNER FROM THE GAME CONSORTIUM'S BUILDING.
STOPPING IS RISKY, BUT WE NEED TO KEEP OUR STRENGTH UP.
PLUS, EVEN WHEN YOU'RE BEING HUNTED ACROSS TOKYO THERE'S NOTHING MORE REFRESHING THAN FRESH STRAWBERRIES AND ICE.
I'VE NEVER SEEN ANYONE DRINK LIKE KILDARE DOES.
HE DOES IT WITH HIS ANTS.
KRIK KRIK KRIK
BUT I GUESS WE ARE ALIENS...
ZCHEEEE
...MAYBE IT'S SOMETHING WE SHOULD CELEBRATE.
SPLOOSH!

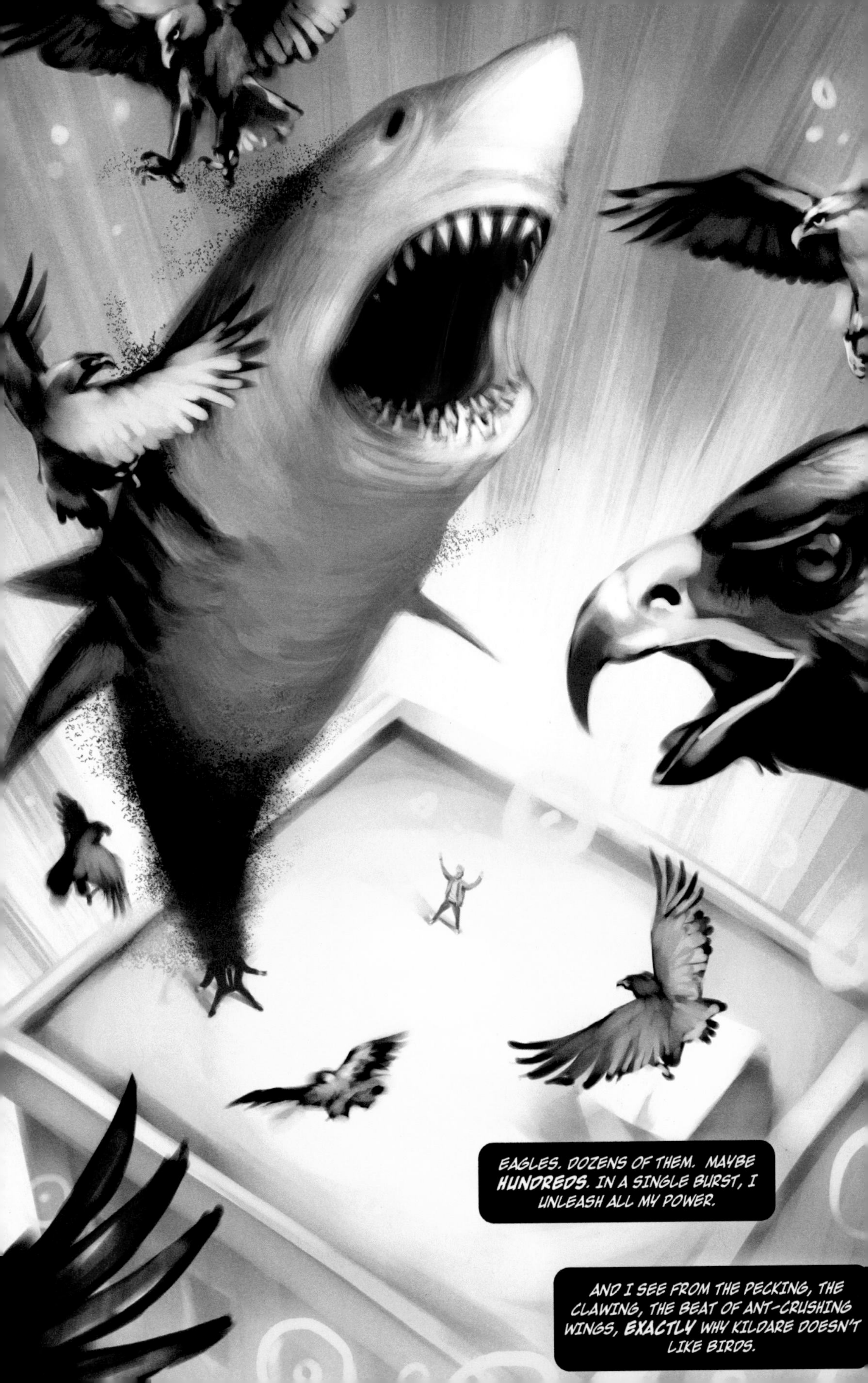
EAGLES. DOZENS OF THEM. MAYBE **HUNDREDS**. IN A SINGLE BURST, I UNLEASH ALL MY POWER.
AND I SEE FROM THE PECKING, THE CLAWING, THE BEAT OF ANT-CRUSHING WINGS, **EXACTLY** WHY KILDARE DOESN'T LIKE BIRDS.

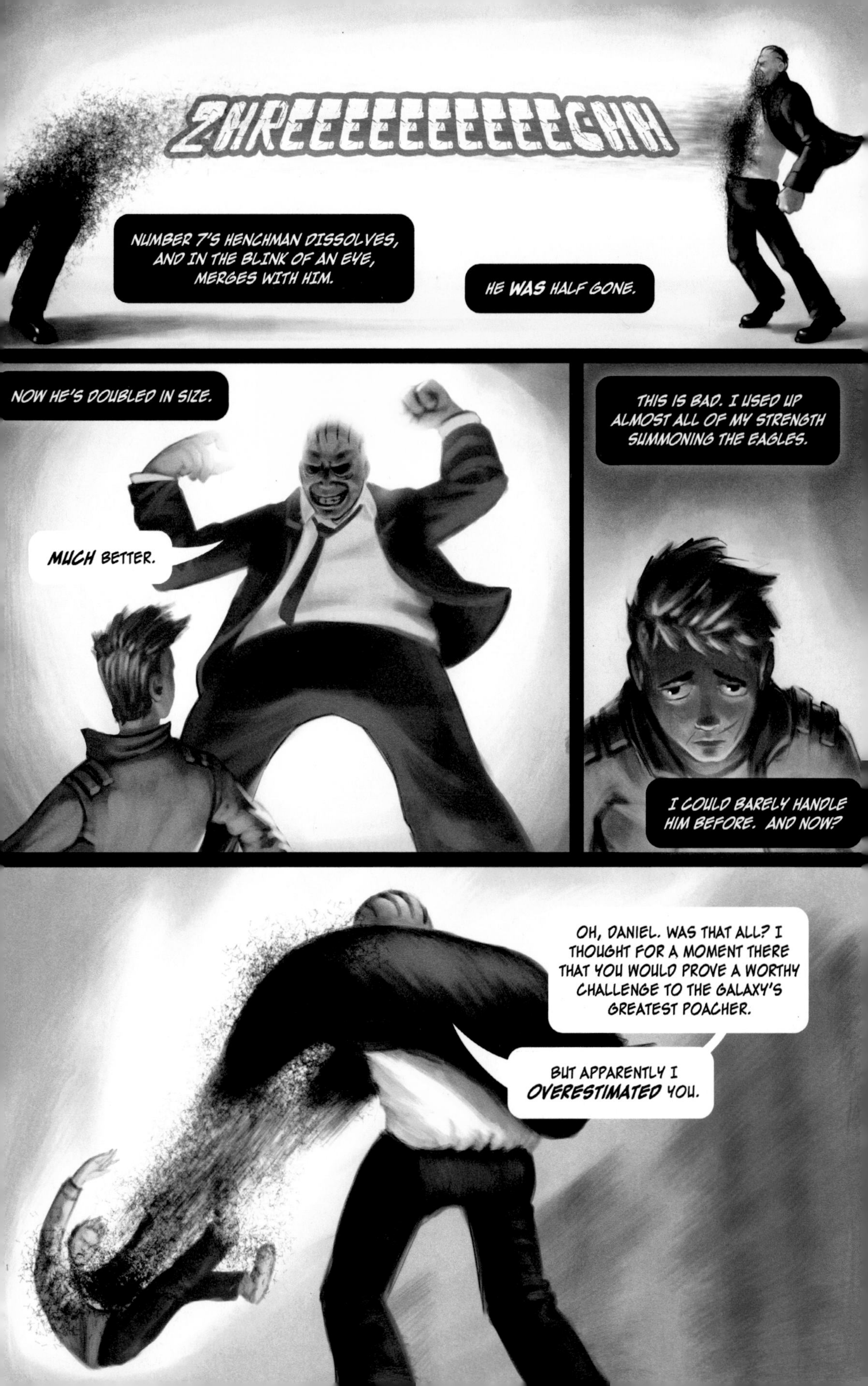
ZHREEEEEEEEEECHH
NUMBER 7'S HENCHMAN DISSOLVES, AND IN THE BLINK OF AN EYE, MERGES WITH HIM.
HE WAS HALF GONE.
NOW HE'S DOUBLED IN SIZE.
MUCH BETTER.
THIS IS BAD. I USED UP ALMOST ALL OF MY STRENGTH SUMMONING THE EAGLES.
I COULD BARELY HANDLE HIM BEFORE. AND NOW?
OH, DANIEL. WAS THAT ALL? I THOUGHT FOR A MOMENT THERE THAT YOU WOULD PROVE A WORTHY CHALLENGE TO THE GALAXY'S GREATEST POACHER.
BUT APPARENTLY I OVERESTIMATED YOU.

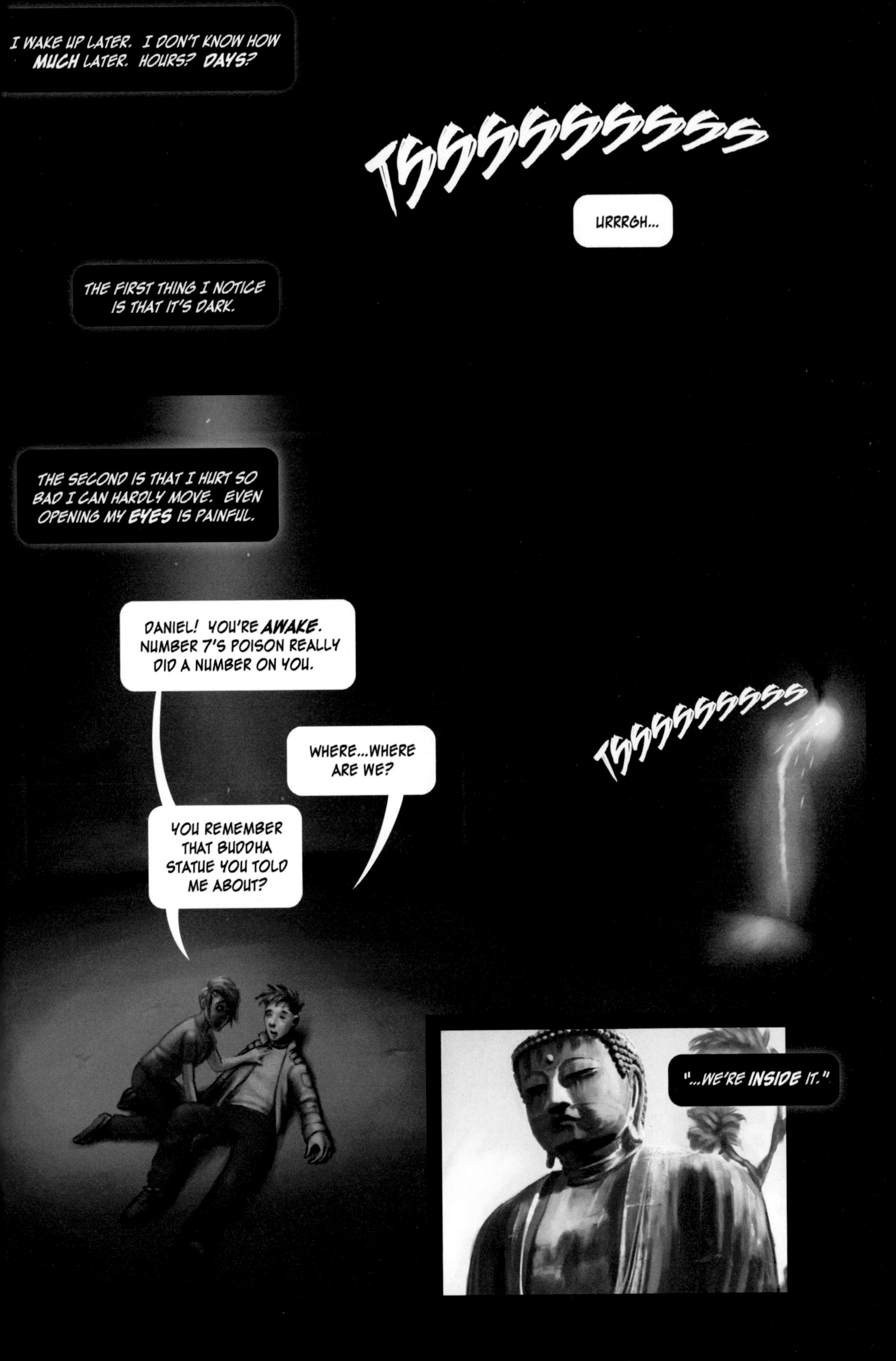

I WAKE UP LATER. I DON'T KNOW HOW MUCH LATER. HOURS? DAYS?
TSSSSSSSSSS
URRRGH...
THE FIRST THING I NOTICE IS THAT IT'S DARK.
THE SECOND IS THAT I HURT SO BAD I CAN HARDLY MOVE. EVEN OPENING MY EYES IS PAINFUL.
DANIEL! YOU'RE AWAKE. NUMBER 7'S POISON REALLY DID A NUMBER ON YOU.
WHERE...WHERE ARE WE?
TSSSSSSSSS
YOU REMEMBER THAT BUDDHA STATUE YOU TOLD ME ABOUT?
"...WE'RE INSIDE IT."

MY HEAD FEELS SO FOGGY, LIKE IT'S FULL OF COTTON. BUT SOMETHING... THERE'S **SOMETHING** I'M FORGETTING...

WAIT! *KILDARE!*

TSSSSSSSSS

I'M...I'M REALLY SORRY, DANIEL. HE'S *GONE.*

WE HAVE TO DISCUSS IT LATER. I THINK IT'S TIME *WE* WERE GONE TOO.

I FINALLY RECOGNIZE THAT HISSING, AND I KNOW SHE'S RIGHT. IT'S THE SOUND OF A WELDING TORCH.

"THIS STATUE HAS KEPT US SAFE FROM NUMBER 7, BUT IT HASN'T STOPPED THE POACHERS, DANIEL. THEY'RE STILL OUT FOR BLOOD."

SOMEONE'S OUTSIDE.

COME ON. WE DON'T HAVE LONG BEFORE THEY BREAK THROUGH.

HER CONFIDENCE IS CONTAGIOUS. BUT THERE ARE STILL SO MANY UNANSWERED QUESTIONS.

DANA...

WE STUMBLE TOGETHER DOWN AN ANCIENT TUNNEL. MY BEST GUESS IS THAT MONKS USED THIS PLACE TO PRAY, HIDDEN FROM THE WORLD.

I DON'T UNDERSTAND? HOW DID WE *GET* HERE? I BLACKED OUT AND...

MY *BRAIN* TELLS ME THAT I CAN BARELY WALK, BUT WITH DANA'S ARM AROUND ME, I DON'T BELIEVE IT. I FEEL LIKE I CAN DO *ANYTHING.*

...YOU WERE *THERE* SOMEHOW.

106

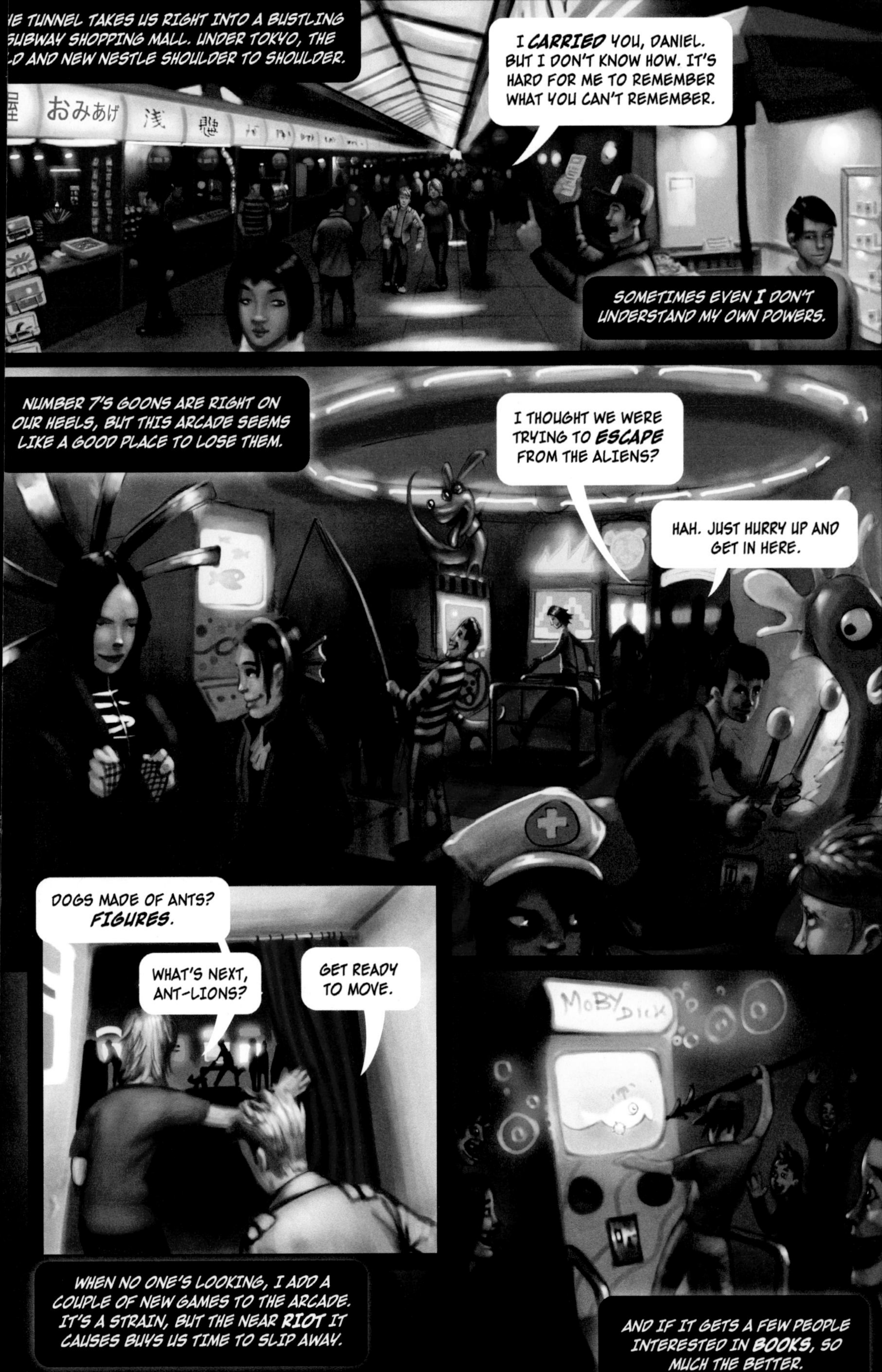
HE TUNNEL TAKES US RIGHT INTO A BUSTLING SUBWAY SHOPPING MALL. UNDER TOKYO, THE LD AND NEW NESTLE SHOULDER TO SHOULDER.
おみあげ
浅
I *CARRIED* YOU, DANIEL. BUT I DON'T KNOW HOW. IT'S HARD FOR ME TO REMEMBER WHAT YOU CAN'T REMEMBER.
SOMETIMES EVEN *I* DON'T UNDERSTAND MY OWN POWERS.
NUMBER 7'S GOONS ARE RIGHT ON OUR HEELS, BUT THIS ARCADE SEEMS LIKE A GOOD PLACE TO LOSE THEM.
I THOUGHT WE WERE TRYING TO **ESCAPE** FROM THE ALIENS?
HAH. JUST HURRY UP AND GET IN HERE.
DOGS MADE OF ANTS? **FIGURES**.
WHAT'S NEXT, ANT-LIONS?
GET READY TO MOVE.
WHEN NO ONE'S LOOKING, I ADD A COUPLE OF NEW GAMES TO THE ARCADE. IT'S A STRAIN, BUT THE NEAR **RIOT** IT CAUSES BUYS US TIME TO SLIP AWAY.
MoBY DICK
AND IF IT GETS A FEW PEOPLE INTERESTED IN **BOOKS**, SO MUCH THE BETTER.

I'M GETTING *TIRED.*

WE RUN THROUGH A "CAPSULE HOTEL." THE ROOMS AREN'T MUCH BIGGER THAN WASHING MACHINES. THERE'S NOT EVEN ROOM TO STAND UP.

THESE GUYS ARE PERSISTENT.

THEY HAVE MY *SCENT,* DANA. WE'RE NOT GOING TO OUTRUN THEM.

WELL, I HOPE YOU HAVE A *BETTER* IDEA THEN.

I'VE ALREADY CARRIED YOU ACROSS HALF OF TOKYO. I DON'T KNOW IF I CAN CARRY YOU ACROSS THE *OTHER* HALF.

WAIT A MINUTE.

WH**OO**M

GOOD THINKING! IF WE CAN *REPROGRAM* IT, MAYBE WE CAN SEND OUT A NEW SIGNAL TO THE POACHERS, ONE THAT WOULD LEAD THEM *AWAY* FROM YOU.

BUT WE'D NEED A WAY TO BROADCAST A SIGNAL TO THE ENTIRE CITY OF TOKYO FROM YOU.

I HAVE SOMETHING IN MIND.

AFTER NUMBER 7 TOOK MY SCENT, HE MUST HAVE SENT IT TO HIS CLIENTS BY COMPUTER, JUST LIKE HE DID WITH THE PLEIONID. THEY'RE TRACKING ME USING *HIS* SIGNAL.

"DO YOU STILL HAVE THAT PDA?"

108

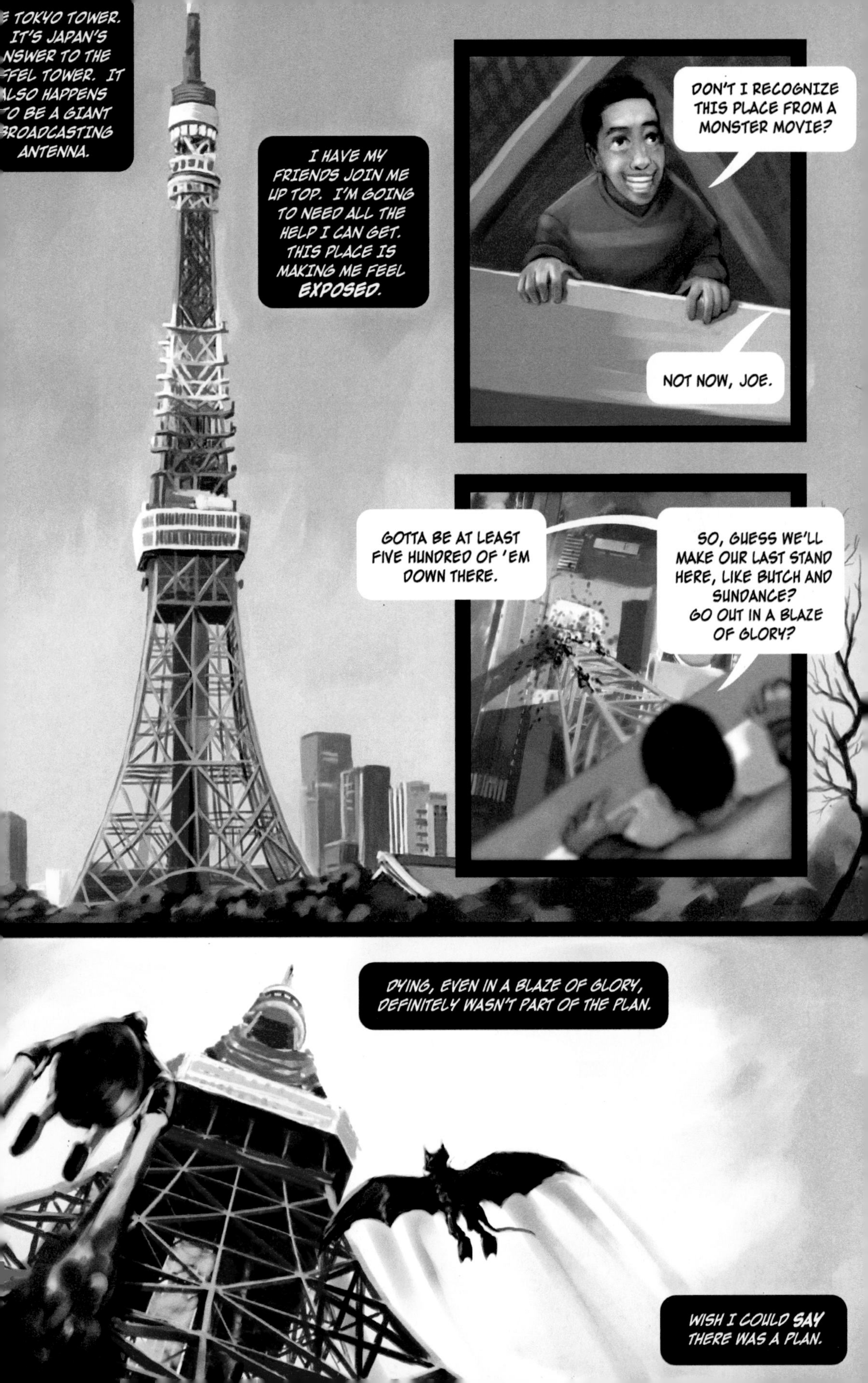
E TOKYO TOWER. IT'S JAPAN'S NSWER TO THE FFEL TOWER. IT ALSO HAPPENS TO BE A GIANT BROADCASTING ANTENNA.
I HAVE MY FRIENDS JOIN ME UP TOP. I'M GOING TO NEED ALL THE HELP I CAN GET. THIS PLACE IS MAKING ME FEEL EXPOSED.
DON'T I RECOGNIZE THIS PLACE FROM A MONSTER MOVIE?
NOT NOW, JOE.
GOTTA BE AT LEAST FIVE HUNDRED OF 'EM DOWN THERE.
SO, GUESS WE'LL MAKE OUR LAST STAND HERE, LIKE BUTCH AND SUNDANCE? GO OUT IN A BLAZE OF GLORY?
DYING, EVEN IN A BLAZE OF GLORY, DEFINITELY WASN'T PART OF THE PLAN.
WISH I COULD SAY THERE WAS A PLAN.

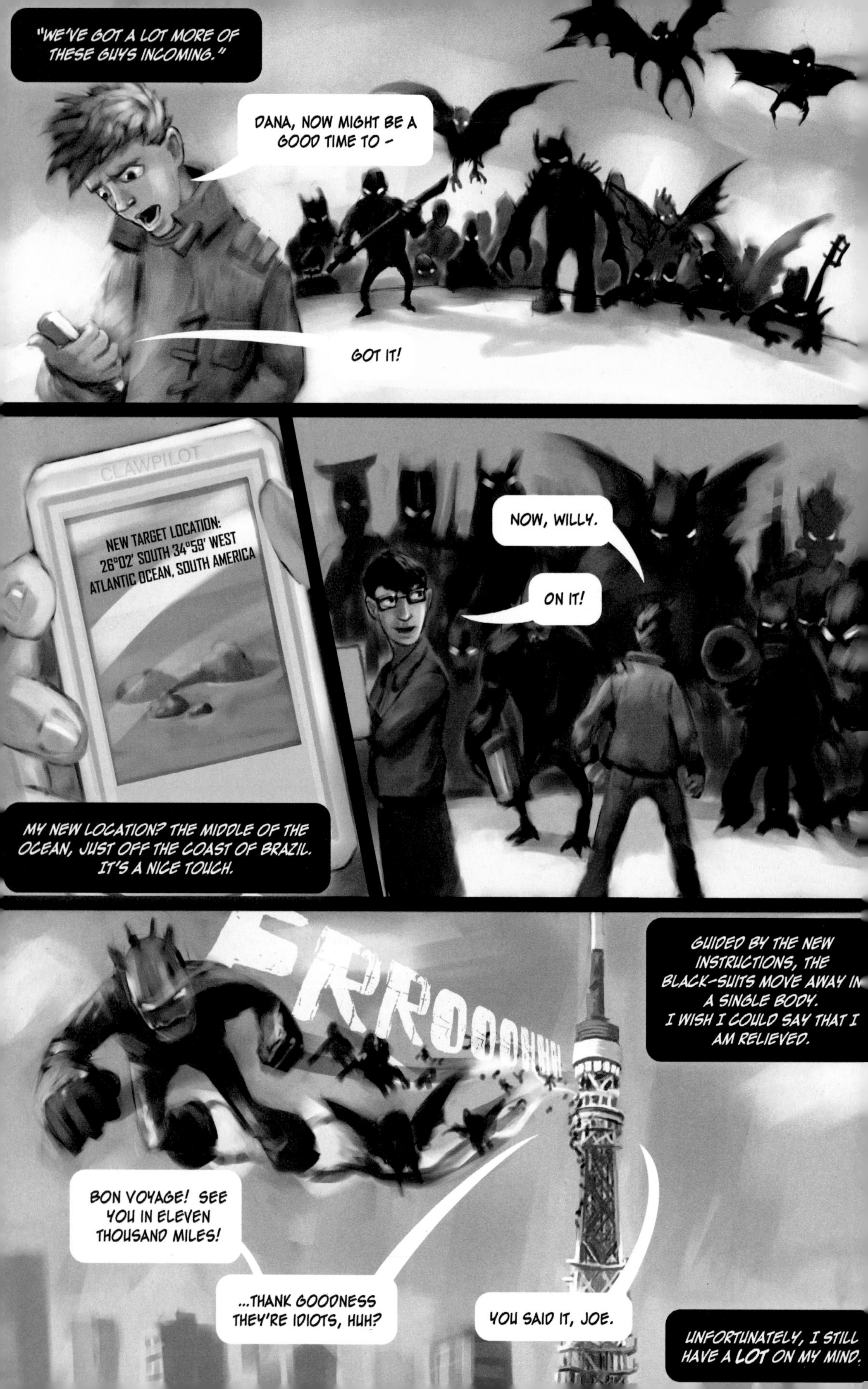
"WE'VE GOT A LOT MORE OF THESE GUYS INCOMING."
DANA, NOW MIGHT BE A GOOD TIME TO -
GOT IT!
CLAWPILOT
NEW TARGET LOCATION: 26°02' SOUTH 34°59' WEST ATLANTIC OCEAN, SOUTH AMERICA
NOW, WILLY.
ON IT!
MY NEW LOCATION? THE MIDDLE OF THE OCEAN, JUST OFF THE COAST OF BRAZIL. IT'S A NICE TOUCH.
SRROOOHHH
GUIDED BY THE NEW INSTRUCTIONS, THE BLACK-SUITS MOVE AWAY IN A SINGLE BODY. I WISH I COULD SAY THAT I AM RELIEVED.
BON VOYAGE! SEE YOU IN ELEVEN THOUSAND MILES!
...THANK GOODNESS THEY'RE IDIOTS, HUH?
YOU SAID IT, JOE.
UNFORTUNATELY, I STILL HAVE A LOT ON MY MIND.

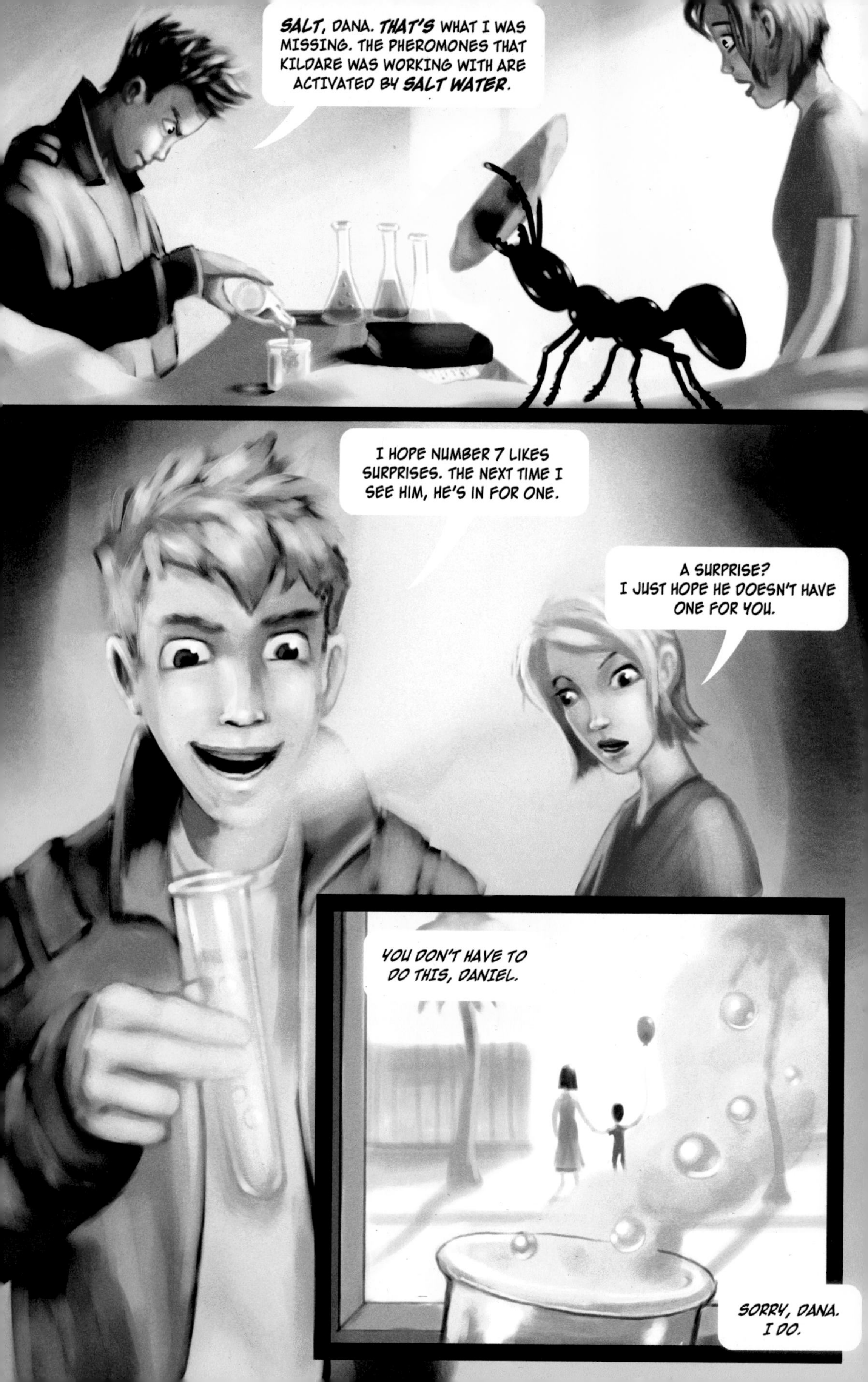
SALT, DANA. THAT'S WHAT I WAS MISSING. THE PHEROMONES THAT KILDARE WAS WORKING WITH ARE ACTIVATED BY SALT WATER.
I HOPE NUMBER 7 LIKES SURPRISES. THE NEXT TIME I SEE HIM, HE'S IN FOR ONE.
A SURPRISE? I JUST HOPE HE DOESN'T HAVE ONE FOR YOU.
YOU DON'T HAVE TO DO THIS, DANIEL.
SORRY, DANA. I DO.

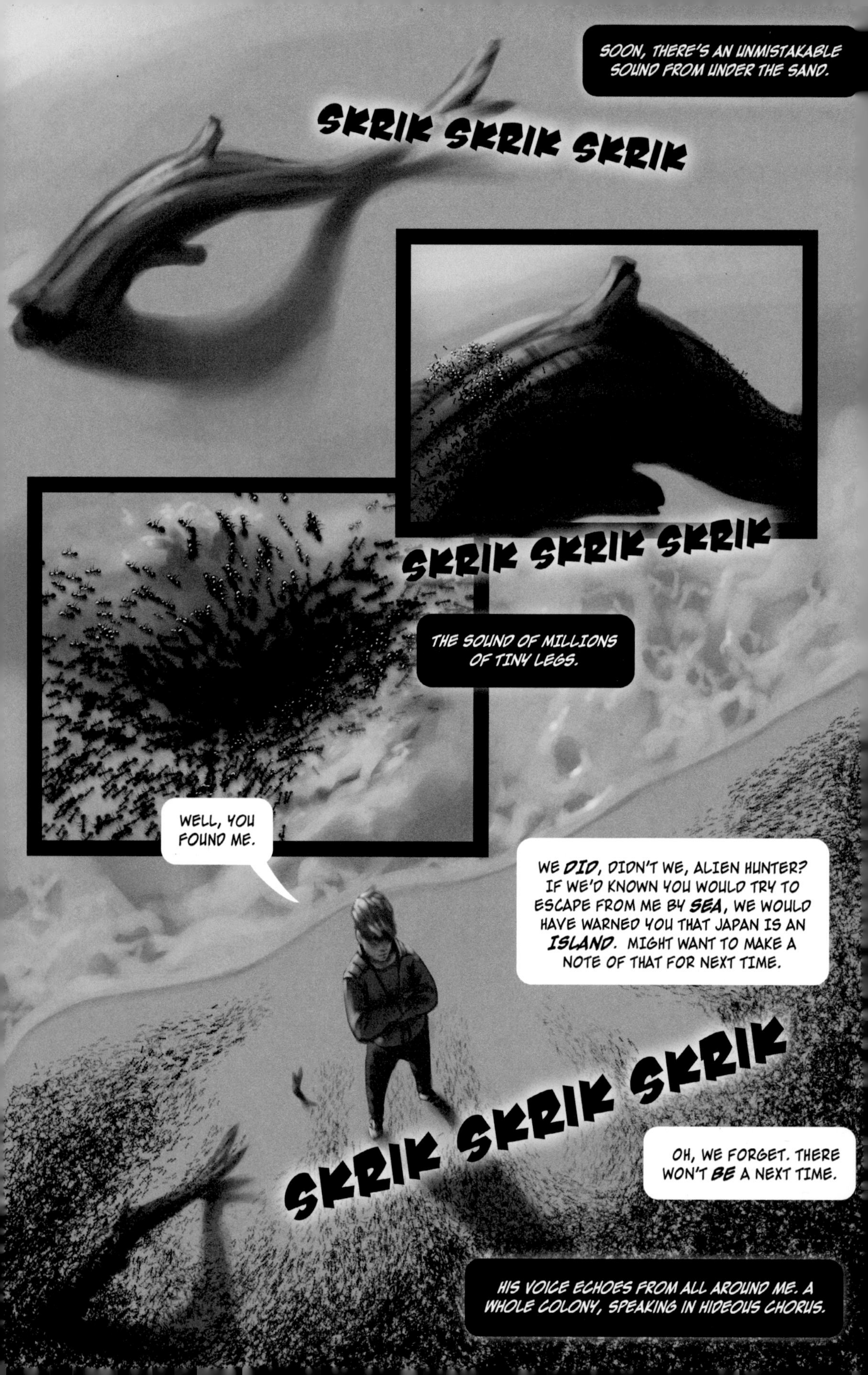
SOON, THERE'S AN UNMISTAKABLE SOUND FROM UNDER THE SAND.
SKRIK SKRIK SKRIK
SKRIK SKRIK SKRIK
THE SOUND OF MILLIONS OF TINY LEGS.
WELL, YOU FOUND ME.
WE DID, DIDN'T WE, ALIEN HUNTER? IF WE'D KNOWN YOU WOULD TRY TO ESCAPE FROM ME BY SEA, WE WOULD HAVE WARNED YOU THAT JAPAN IS AN ISLAND. MIGHT WANT TO MAKE A NOTE OF THAT FOR NEXT TIME.
SKRIK SKRIK SKRIK
OH, WE FORGET. THERE WON'T BE A NEXT TIME.
HIS VOICE ECHOES FROM ALL AROUND ME. A WHOLE COLONY, SPEAKING IN HIDEOUS CHORUS.

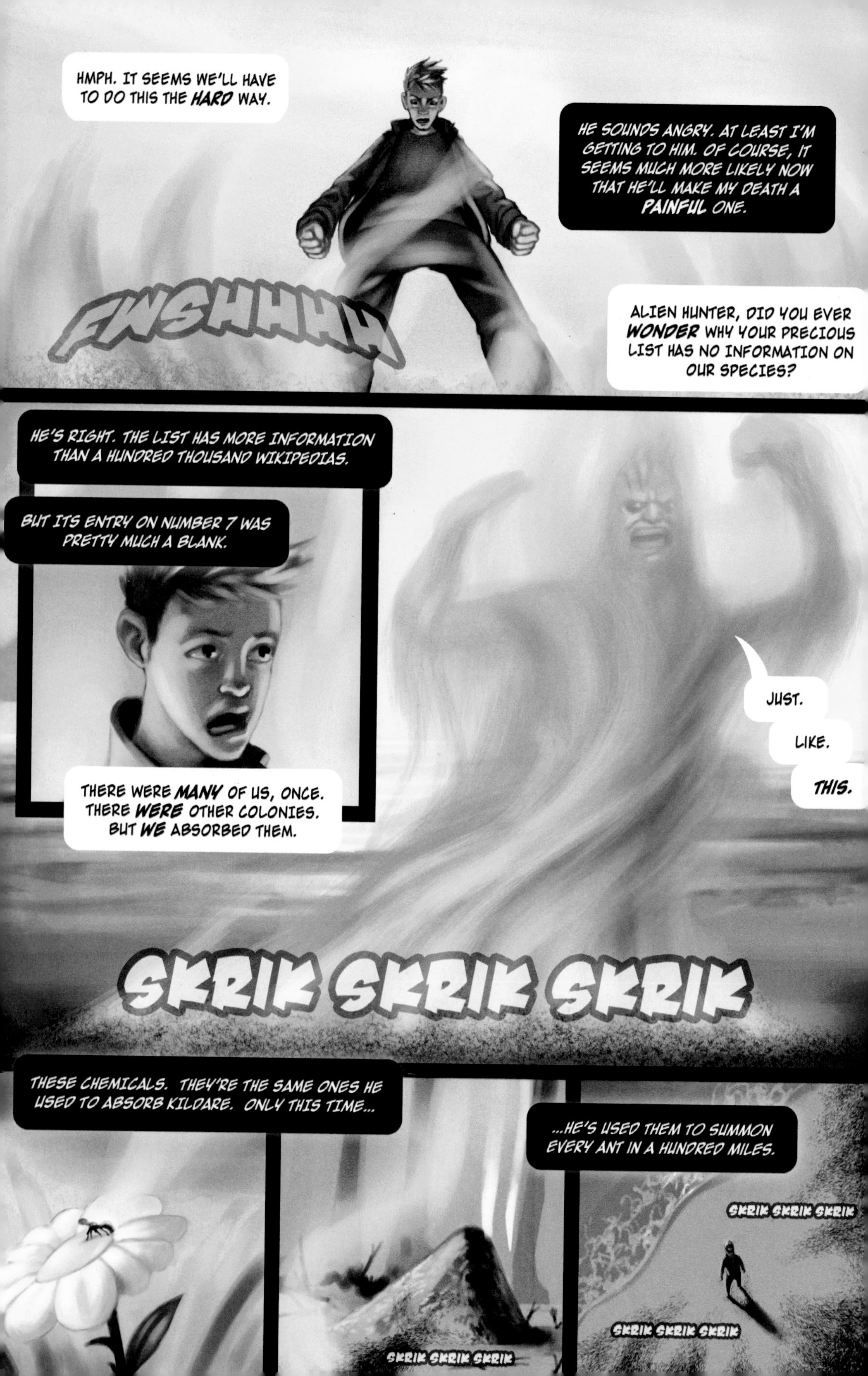
HMPH. IT SEEMS WE'LL HAVE TO DO THIS THE HARD WAY.
HE SOUNDS ANGRY. AT LEAST I'M GETTING TO HIM. OF COURSE, IT SEEMS MUCH MORE LIKELY NOW THAT HE'LL MAKE MY DEATH A PAINFUL ONE.
FWSHHHH
ALIEN HUNTER, DID YOU EVER WONDER WHY YOUR PRECIOUS LIST HAS NO INFORMATION ON OUR SPECIES?
HE'S RIGHT. THE LIST HAS MORE INFORMATION THAN A HUNDRED THOUSAND WIKIPEDIAS.
BUT ITS ENTRY ON NUMBER 7 WAS PRETTY MUCH A BLANK.
THERE WERE MANY OF US, ONCE. THERE WERE OTHER COLONIES. BUT WE ABSORBED THEM.
JUST.
LIKE.
THIS.
SKRIK SKRIK SKRIK
THESE CHEMICALS. THEY'RE THE SAME ONES HE USED TO ABSORB KILDARE. ONLY THIS TIME...
...HE'S USED THEM TO SUMMON EVERY ANT IN A HUNDRED MILES.
SKRIK SKRIK SKRIK
SKRIK SKRIK SKRIK
SKRIK SKRIK SKRIK

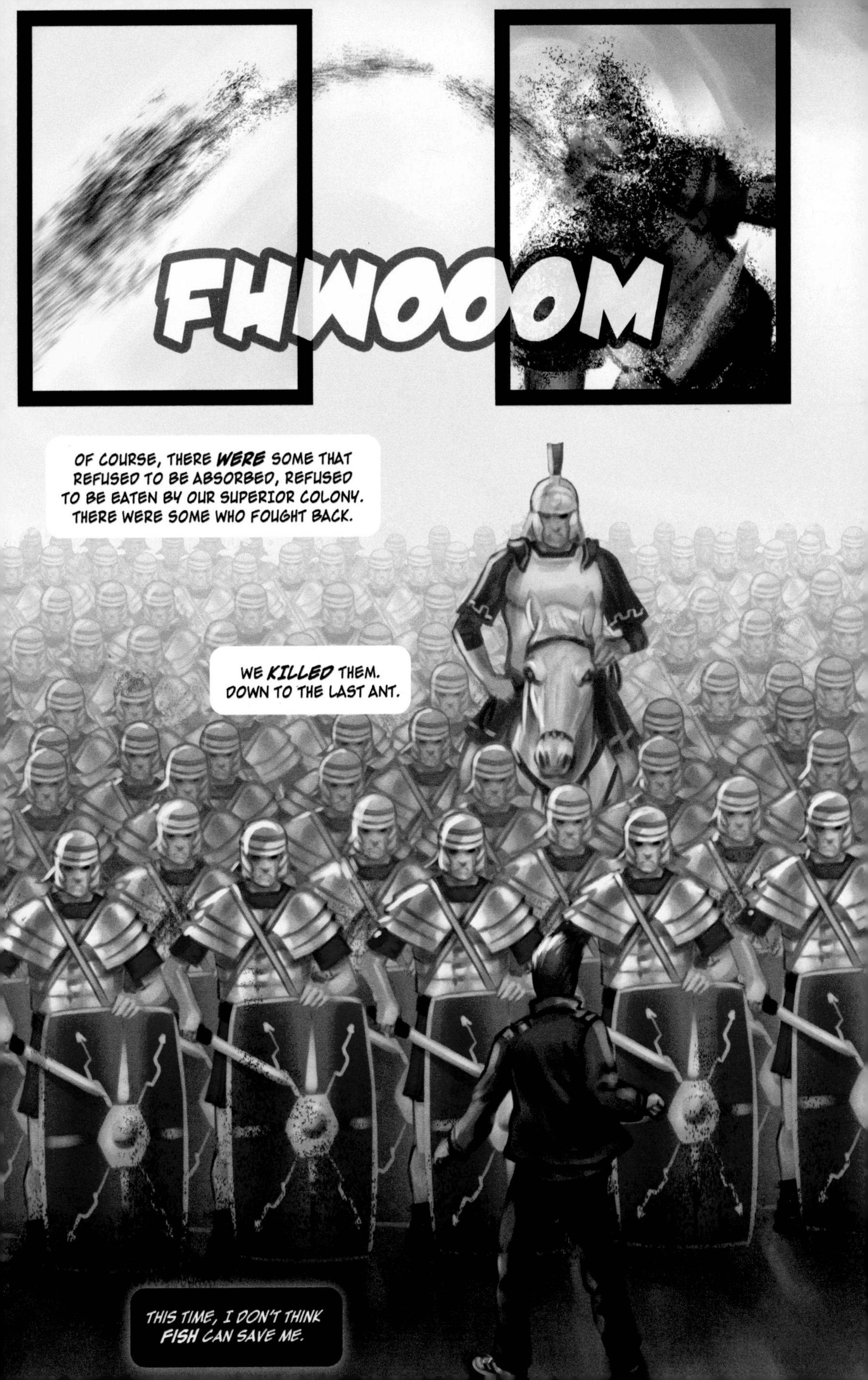
FHWOOOM
OF COURSE, THERE WERE SOME THAT REFUSED TO BE ABSORBED, REFUSED TO BE EATEN BY OUR SUPERIOR COLONY. THERE WERE SOME WHO FOUGHT BACK.
WE KILLED THEM. DOWN TO THE LAST ANT.
THIS TIME, I DON'T THINK FISH CAN SAVE ME.

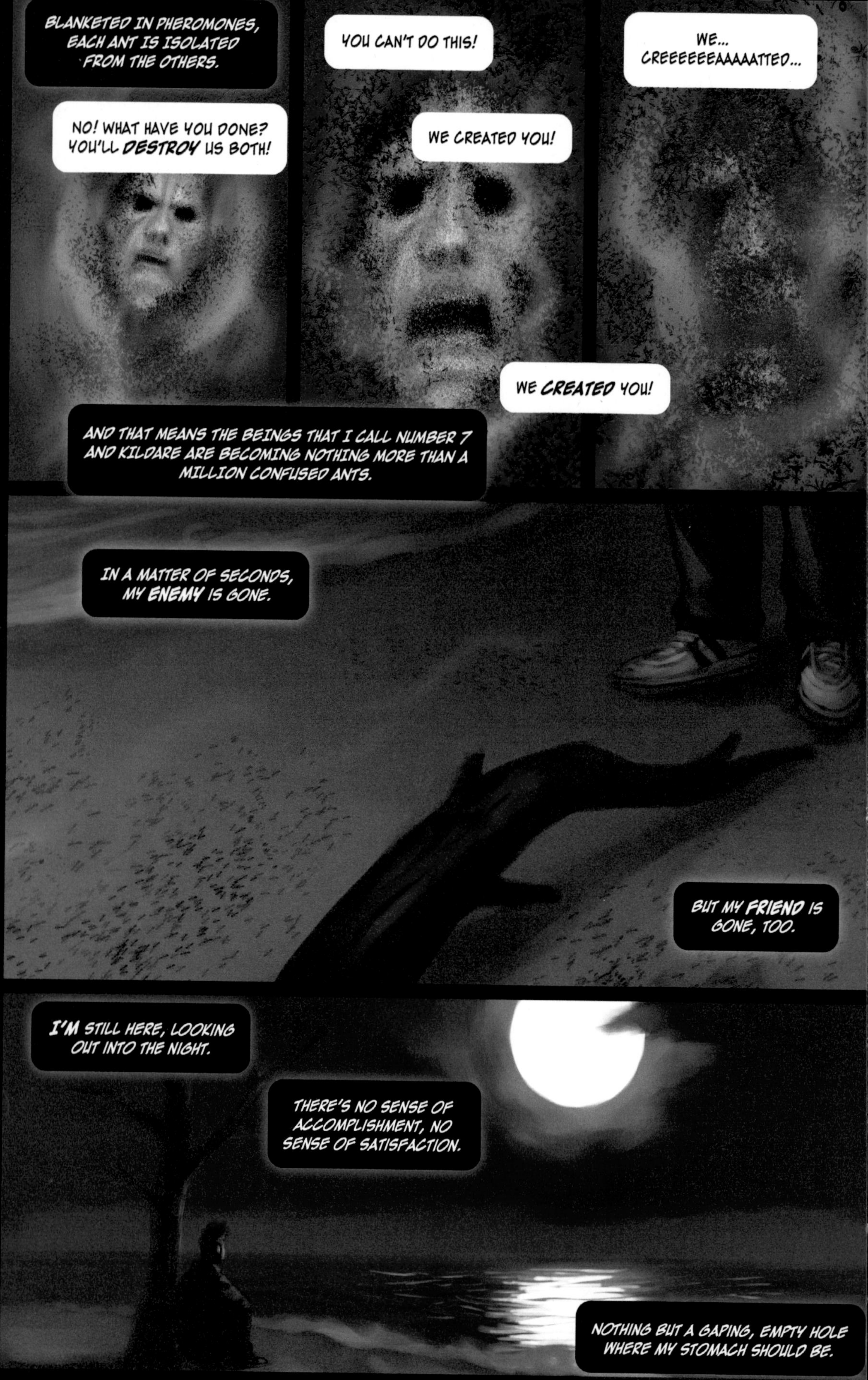

BLANKETED IN PHEROMONES, EACH ANT IS ISOLATED FROM THE OTHERS.

YOU CAN'T DO THIS!

WE... CREEEEEEAAAAATTED...

NO! WHAT HAVE YOU DONE? YOU'LL *DESTROY* US BOTH!

WE CREATED YOU!

WE *CREATED* YOU!

AND THAT MEANS THE BEINGS THAT I CALL NUMBER 7 AND KILDARE ARE BECOMING NOTHING MORE THAN A MILLION CONFUSED ANTS.

IN A MATTER OF SECONDS, MY *ENEMY* IS GONE.

BUT MY *FRIEND* IS GONE, TOO.

I'M STILL HERE, LOOKING OUT INTO THE NIGHT.

THERE'S NO SENSE OF ACCOMPLISHMENT, NO SENSE OF SATISFACTION.

NOTHING BUT A GAPING, EMPTY HOLE WHERE MY STOMACH SHOULD BE.

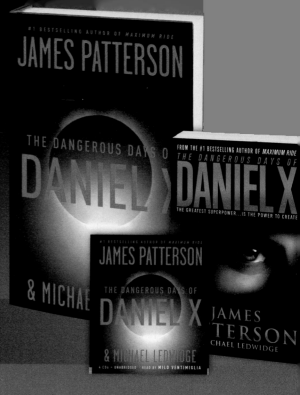